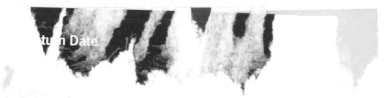

RESEARCH HIGHLIGHTS
IN SOCIAL WORK

Approaches to Addiction

RESEARCH HIGHLIGHTS IN SOCIAL WORK

APPROACHES TO ADDICTION

St. Martin's Press
New York

Editor: Joyce Lishman
Secretary: Margaret Donald
Editorial Advisory Committee:

Professor G. Rochford	University of Aberdeen
Dr P. Seed	University of Aberdeen
Dr A. Robertson	University of Edinburgh
Mr P. Hambleton	Central Region Social Work Department (SSRG Scotland Chairman)
Mr S. Montgomery	Grampian Region Social Work Department
Mr M. Brown	Highland Region Social Work Department
Mr J. Tibbitt	Social Work Services Group

University of Aberdeen
Department of Social Work
Kings College
Aberdeen

Printed in Great Britain

First published in the United States of America in 1985
Library of Congress Catalog Card Number 85 - 40082

ISBN 0-312-04647-2

LIST OF CONTENTS

Contributors

Joyce Lishman

Her Ph.D. research at Aberdeen University analyses social workers' behaviour in interviews using videotapes and explores the relationship between this behaviour and prognosis and outcome. Previously a social worker in child and adolescent psychiatry. Publications include 'A Clash in Perspective? A Study of Worker and Client Perceptions of Social Work' *British Journal of Social Work*, 8, 3, 1974, a study of her own practice.

Mike Ashton

Mike Ashton has been an Information Officer at the library of the Institute for the Study of Drug Dependence since 1975. He is currently responsible for the library's publications programme which aims to provide social welfare practitioners with basic information about drug misuse in Britain.

Bill Saunders

Senior Lecturer/Director, Alcohol Studies Centre, Paisley College of Technology. Previously a clinical psychologist working in an Alcohol Treatment Unit in Glasgow. His current duties include being Director of Studies for the Post-graduate Diploma in Alcohol Studies Course, which is a C.C.E.T.S.W. approved post-qualifying course, and designing in-service education programmes for professional and voluntary workers. In 1984 he was a W.H.O. Consultant to South East Asia and was also seconded to the Western Australian Alcohol and Drug Authority to advise on the establishment of alcohol education programmes for professional workers.

Jim Orford

Jim Orford trained as a clinical psychologist at the Maudsley Hospital/Institute of Psychiatry and returned there to work between 1966 and 1976 as research psychologist in the Addiction Research Unit where his research included a major study of married couples with drinking problems. He now has a joint University/Health Service appointment in Exeter, is a member of the Exeter Community Alcohol Team and responsible for clinical psychology training and research. Amongst his published work is the book *Alcohol and the Family* co-

	edited with Judith Harwin, and a book *Excessive Appetites: A Psychology of Addiction* will appear in 1984 or 1985.
Rowdy Yates	Project Co-ordinator of Lifeline Project (An Independent Drugs Advice/Training Resource). A member of Standing Conference on Drug Abuse (SCODA), Manchester District Drugs Advisory Committee, and North West Regional Drug Problem Team. Publications include 'An Experiment in Multi-Facility Induction' Proceedings of the 4th World Conference on Therapeutic Communities, New York, 1979; 'Out of the Shadows', NACRO, London, 1981; 'The Organisation of a Street-Level Crisis Centre: An Abstract of Addiction', CURR Discussion Paper No. 9, University of Glasgow, 1983; 'Non-Voluntary Admission to Treatment Programmes' (with Dr. J. Strang) Council of Europe, (Pompidou Group) Strasburg, 1983.
Stewart Asquith	Lecturer in the Department of Social Administration at the University of Edinburgh. He has written a number of articles in the field of juvenile justice. His main publications are *Discretion and Welfare* edited with M. Adler, Heinemann 1981; *Children and Justice* Edinburgh University Press 1983; and *Social Work and Social Philosophy* with Chris Clark, RKP, 1984.
Elizabeth Jagger	Research student in the Department of Social Administration at the University of Edinburgh where she tutors in Social Administration. She also tutors in Sociology at the University of Stirling. She is currently interviewing families of children who have used solvents.
Ewan MacLean	Research Associate in the Centre for Criminology and the Social and Philosophical Study of Law, University of Edinburgh, and currently employed on a survey of crime and its control in Scotland over the last twenty five years. He has participated and assisted in two E.E.C. higher education comparative study programmes which investigated alcohol and drugs control policies in a number of European countries. He is also presently completing a Ph.D. thesis on the development and social meaning of art forgery, which combines his interests in criminology with those in the sociology and history of art.

EDITORIAL

Joyce Lishman

In choosing titles for the Research Highlights series one aim has been relevance and topicality. *Approaches to Addiction* is certainly topical. The recent release of the Home Office statistics on The Misuse of Drugs[1] has been accompanied by a proliferation of reportage in both the popular and social work press on addiction, particularly on heroin abuse and glue sniffing.[2]

The intention in commissioning this volume was twofold:

1.   to review critically research on the place and meaning of addictions in current society.

2.   to draw implications from research on addictions for the policy maker, manager or practitioner trying to deal with the consequences of such an addiction.

The volume begins with a review of research and statistical evidence about the extent of medical and non-medical use of psychotropic drugs in Britain, including not only opiates, LSD and cannabis, but alcohol, tobacco and caffeine and the medical use of psychotropic drugs such as benzodiazepines (tranquillisers). Specific chapters then deal with approaches to solvent abuse and addiction to alcohol and hard drugs, but not with addiction to tobacco, or to benzodiazepine although the latter omission is not by intention; no contributor was available. Although concern about tranquilliser addiction is rising[3] recognition of this problem is more recent than of other 'addictions'. Research evidence about its nature and treatment is correspondingly more limited [4][5][6].

The resulting volume, read as a whole, is paradoxical and may prove frustrating to practitioners, managers and policy makers concerned to *act* on the basis of research implications.

The problematic nature of the volume arises for at least two reasons: differences in perception of the nature of the problem and in the availability of conclusive evidence about effective treatment.

In the field of alcohol abuse, as Saunders and Orford both describe, there is not only agreement that there is a problem but a well-established base of research on the effectiveness of intervention which has led to changes in practice, from an expensive psycho-dynamic individual treatment approach to one which relies more on self-help and community programmes.

In the field of heroin and solvent abuse, however, there is considerably less agreement on what sort of problem abuse constitutes: for example, contrast Edwards and Busch's view[7] that there is evidence that drug problems are out of control with the approach of Yates, Asquith and MacLean in this volume questioning such an interpretation. Secondly, and partly as a consequence of the lack of agreement or paradigm about the nature of the problem in these fields, the research into effectiveness of treatment is less extensive and correspondingly less conclusive.

The approach of Asquith and MacLean questions the appropriateness of intense public concern about heroin and solvent abuse in contrast to public attitudes of acceptance of alcohol and tobacco abuse and highlights political and social implications of the differences in concern. While this approach may be frustrating for a practitioner faced with what to do *now* with a client, it is an essential component of any overview of research on addiction.

The approach does also have relevance to practice. Public attitudes of concern and horror at hard drug abuse have contributed to a mystification of this problem and client group whereby practitioners become deskilled, having difficulty in applying their general understanding of work with clients with social and emotional difficulties to hard drug abusers, and consigning them to a specialist category, e.g. only to be dealt with by the medical profession. Analysis of addiction as part of wider social issues, particularly of control and access to resources, has different implications for action than analysis of addiction based on an individual illness model.

We hope this volume, in spite of its limitations, will stimulate the reader to greater awareness of the social and political implications of addiction as well as drawing out some practice and policy implications for working with addicted clients.

References

1. Home Office.
2. See for example: 'Heroin: Stemming the Tide' *Sunday Times.* 19 August 1984, p.15.

   'Drug Abuse: Shooting Up' *The Economist.* 18 August 1984. Vernon, L. 'Addiction is now manifesting as a crisis for society' *Social Work Today.* 10 September 1984.

   'Anger over glue study' Currents, *Social Work Today.* 2 September 1984.
3. Medical Research Council *Annual Report* 1982-3. 20 Park Crescent, London, W1N 4AL.
4. Lader, M. 'Benzodiazepines - panacea or poison' *Australia and New Zealand Journal of Psychiatry.* 15(1) 1982, 1-9.
5. Lader, M. & Petursson, M. 'Benzodiazepine derivatives - side effects and dangers' *Biological Psychiatry.* 16(12) 1981, 1195-1201
6. Tyrer, P. 'Clinical and Pharmacological evidence of dependence on Benzodiazepine hypnotics' *in* Nicholson, A.N. *Hypnotics in Clinical Practice.* Proceedings of a symposium held in Edinburgh, May 1982. Medicine Publishing Foundation, Oxford, 1982, 59-66.
7. Edwards, G. & Busch, G. (Eds.) *Drug Problems in Britain: A Review of Ten Years.* Academic Press, London, 1981.

An invaluable source of information on addiction is:

The Institute for the Study of Drug Dependence
Library and Information Service
Kingsbury House
3 Blackburn Road
London NW6 1XA

Surveys and Statistics on Drugtaking in Britain*

Mike Ashton

INTRODUCTION

This paper summarises some of the available research and statistical information about the extent of medical and non-medical use of psychotropic (affecting the mind) drugs in Britain and is divided into six sections. The first two sections are about the extent of drug 'misuse'. Unfortunately, this term has no accepted definition. It refers here to forms of drugtaking which attract social disapproval, and which 'society' as a whole actively discourages. The most clear-cut instances involve drugs whose possession for non-medical use has actually been made illegal under the Misuse of Drugs Act (like opiates, LSD, amphetamines, cannabis). But - where this exists - information on the non-medical use of substances (like solvents) which are subject to different kinds of restriction, has been included. Part 1 is about surveys of drug misuse in the general population; part 2, about official statistics relating to the misuse of drugs.

The third section looks at the extent of socially accepted forms of recreational drugtaking, involving drugs like alcohol, tobacco and caffeine, whose non-medical use society permits, and permits to be encouraged. Set against these, drug misuse can be seen as one relatively limited feature of what is without doubt, a drug-using society.

*This paper is reprinted from an ISDD publication and the different original focus is reflected in minor differences in the system of referencing and general format from the usual style of Research Highlights.

We are grateful to Mike Ashton for providing this paper, at extremely short notice, when the original contributor failed to deliver his paper on the epidemiology of addiction.

All sources for the information are available from the author, ISDD, 1-4 Hatton Place, Hatton Garden, London EC1N 8ND; 01-430-1991. Copyright is with the Institute for the Study of Drug Dependence.

The fourth section concerns the level of the medical use of psychotropic drugs. This information is, indirectly, very relevant to the non-medical use or misuse of the same drugs.

The fifth section uses the information in the previous section to attempt a synthesis summarising what is known, estimated or guessed about the extent of drug use in Britain. The final section refers to the most important sources used in compiling this review.

Drug Use and Drug Misuse

The divisions between the first four sections are, to some extent, artificial. In the 'real world' socially acceptable and socially unacceptable drugtaking do not exist in isolation, but are interconnected at a number of levels. At a 'philosophical' level, it is often argued that pervasive socially accepted drug use encourages people to see drugtaking as an appropriate way of responding to personal or social difficulties, or simply to the desire to alter mood. This theory would suggest that extensive use of medicines, alcohol, tobacco, etc, lowers psychological barriers to drug misuse.

More prosaically, the same people who misuse drugs may also use medicines or alcohol as part of a pattern of dependent drugtaking, or to achieve the same state of sedation or stimulation. This crossover is seen most clearly with opioid addicts. Once in treatment, they may receive a prescription for the same drug they had previously 'misused' and obtained through the illicit market; in both cases, the addict may be using the drug for the same purposes from their point of view - to stave off withdrawal, to get 'high', to dull the senses. Statistically, their prescriptions will be counted in table 9, a table to do with medical drug use, and will also cause the patient to appear as an addict 'receiving drugs as at 31 December' in table 1, a table usually considered under the heading of the misuse of drugs.

SURVEYS OF DRUG MISUSE

'How many people misuse drugs in the UK?' is a deceptively simple question without any satisfactory answer - the necessary information just does not exist. Official statistics on drug misuse (a selection of which are reproduced in part 2) are part of the answer. However, all these statistics rely on drug misusers or drug misuse incidents somehow coming to the attention of the authorities, and no-one knows for sure what proportion these are of the total number. For more directly relevant information, we must turn to sample surveys and other research methodologies that reach beyond official counts of people coming to notice.

Representative National Surveys

The only satisfactory way of estimating the number of persons 'misusing' drugs would be to conduct reliable, large-scale, representative and confidential surveys of the general population, surveys carefully designed to elicit the required information. No such survey has ever been done.

There are two national surveys which included questions on drug misuse, but neither meets all these criteria. The first was done in 1969 by the government's Office of Population Censuses and Surveys (OPCS). It found that about 5% of the adult (aged 16-69) population of England and Wales admitted to ever having used 'illegal' drugs. Most, 4% of the sample, had used 'pep-pills' (amphetamines), just over 2% had used cannabis, and less than 0.5% each had used LSD, cocaine or heroin. But this survey was designed primarily to investigate public attitudes to drugtaking, and the sample was not large enough to give accurate estimates of the relatively small numbers of people who had actually used drugs.

The second national survey was done in 1973 for the BBC, and asked a sample of adults in the UK whether they had ever used drugs for non-medical purposes. It found, in inner London, that nearly half the sample aged between 17 and 34 years said that they had used cannabis, whilst in rural areas just over a quarter said they had done so. Overall, the study suggested that some 3.8 million people in the UK had ever used cannabis, nearly 1.3 million had used amphetamines, 650,000 had used LSD, and nearly 600,000 had used sleeping pills. But once again the sample size was too small (and there were other shortcomings) for these results to be relied upon.

Also neither of these surveys provides information about whether people who said they had used drugs were continuing to use them, nor how heavy their drug use was. So the figures they come up with will lump together people who had used drugs once or twice some time ago, along with those who are currently heavy users.

Selective and Local Surveys

Complementing these national surveys, there are a number of surveys of people in a particular area, or of a particular age/social status, but these have usually been conducted independently of each other, using different methods, and asking differently phrased questions, so results are difficult to compare.

Schools

One survey of 14-18 year-old school children conducted in 1973 by ISDD, did sample on a national basis, but is listed in this section because the 70 English schools included in the study were not selected to be representative of the total school population. Overall, about 9% of the pupils reported having taken drugs, increasing with age from 6% amongst the fourth-formers to 12% amongst sixth-formers. Less than half of these (4% of the total sample) had used drugs on more than three occasions.

About 7% of the ISDD sample had used cannabis, making it by far the most popular drug. About 2% each had used sedatives, stimulants or LSD, and practically none had taken opiates, cocaine or solvents. A partial replication of the study carried out a year later reported a similar picture, and emphasised the variation between schools, ranging from one where nearly half the pupils said they had used drugs, to several where none at all said they had done so.

Other surveys generally confirm that about 10% of secondary school pupils aged 14-plus have used drugs other than alcohol or tobacco, with (in the 1970s) cannabis being most popular, followed by amphetamines and LSD, and with vanishingly small proportions ever having used opiates or cocaine. They also (not surprisingly) reveal higher rates of ever having used drugs amongst older pupils; one study of 16-17 year olds in Glasgow suggested that as many as 1 in 8 of the sample had used LSD. The studies also agree that 'regular' use is very infrequent (less than 5%), and reflect the local variability noted in the national surveys.

All these surveys were conducted before 1975, and therefore before the present wave of concern over the incidence of solvent misuse. A survey of one Glasgow boys' school indicated increasing prevalence of solvent misuse over the years 1976-1982. By 1982, between 20-25% of pupils aged 13-15 admitted to having misused solvents, and 13% had done so on more than one occasion.

The most recent survey of illegal drug use amongst school children was conducted in the winter of 1979/80 in five schools in the Lothian region of Scotland. It found that 15% of boys and 11% of girls aged 15-16 reported ever having used drugs for 'kicks' or out of curiosity. Most commonly used was cannabis (7%), then tranquillisers (5%), solvents (nearly 5%), and amphetamines (2.5%). About 1% each reported having taken LSD, heroin or cocaine.

Students

University level students are the single most studied group in the general population. Studies done in the early '70s suggest that characteristically about a third of students had ever misused drugs, ranging in different colleges and locations from 10 to 40%. Experience of drug use was more common amongst students in the social sciences, arts and medicine, less common amongst business and physical science students, and increased with the amount of time in further education. Almost all students who had tried drugs had tried amphetamines and the same proportion had tried LSD, whilst just 1 in 100 had experience of heroin.

Except for cannabis, information on the frequency of student drug use is very sparse. With respect to cannabis, about 60-70% of the students who had ever used it saw themselves as continuing to use it, and 20-25% were using it at least once a week. So on average 6-9% of all students in higher education used cannabis weekly.

Some evidence that the situation is not likely to have changed very much since the early '70s is contained in a more recent report on a London polytechnic. The researchers found that the proportions of new students who had tried various drugs had changed relatively little between 1970 and 1978. In 1978, nearly 30% had tried cannabis, 15% amphetamines, 6% each had tried LSD or cocaine, whilst practically none had tried heroin.

Local Surveys

The remaining studies investigating 'normal' populations (as opposed to selected groups of offenders, psychiatric patients, addicts etc) are confined to the residents of a particular area, but these generally relied on research methods other than survey techniques. As such most are difficult to compare with the results already cited. The few surveys that have been done confirm that cannabis is the most popular of the drugs, having been used by three-quarters or more of the people who have ever misused drugs; amphetamines are next, followed by a small minority who have used LSD, and practically none who have used opiates.

On average, the results suggest that about 15% of young people not in further education had misused drugs controlled under the Misuse of Drugs Act, though again most of these studies date from the early or mid '70s.

The most recent (and as yet unpublished) survey of this kind was conducted in the early '80s and followed up a group of schoolchildren first investigated in 1979/80 (see earlier section on Schools). By the time they were aged 19-20, 37% of the men and 23% of the women had tried drugs (including solvents and tranquillisers used for non-medical purposes), mainly cannabis. Fewer than 1% had ever tried heroin. Rates of drug misuse were higher among the unemployed.

Drug Abuse 'Indicators' Studies

Some studies have used a combination of the records of the various agencies with which dependent drug users, or drug users in difficulty, might have contact, as a means of assessing the prevalence of drug problems in a particular area. These agencies might include the probation and social services, hospitals, doctors, police, solicitors, advice centres, specialist drug agencies, etc.

One such study in Bristol during 1971-73 estimated a peak prevalence rate for addicted drug injectors of less than 1 (0.68) in every 1,000 of the local population aged 15-29. Another estimated that, in 1975, just over 1 in every 1,000 of the London population aged 15-65 attended casualty departments with a problem arising from their drug dependence.

More recent research into the extent of problematic drug use in two inner London boroughs suggests that at some time during 1983 about 17 per 1,000 of the population aged 16-44 used opioids on a daily or almost daily basis, and were presumably to some degree dependent. At any time the number will have been smaller, perhaps 10 in every 1,000. Most will have been using illegally imported heroin. The authors suggest that at least as many again may have experienced problems arising from their misuse of drugs other than opioids.

A similar study in South Tyneside in 1981 identified at least 142 people misusing drugs in the area, a minimal prevalence rate of 2.3 per 1,000 of the local population aged 16-44. This is over 4 times the number of known notified addicts in South Tyneside. Of the people identified, about 60% were found to be experiencing a variety of problems due to their drug use. The majority of drug misusers took opiates, and many also took other drugs. However, the authors caution that the method used in this study does not reveal the actual prevalence of problem drug taking, which is certainly greater than the figure quoted above.

In the County of Avon, an indicators-type study identified 304 young solvent misusers during a 6 month period in 1981, a prevalence rate of about 2.1 per 1,000 of the county's population aged 10 to 19.

It should be stressed that all these studies rely heavily on drugtakers coming to the notice of various agencies and authorities.

OFFICIAL STATISTICS ON THE MISUSE OF DRUGS

The official statistics on the misuse of drugs reproduced below ultimately derive from two sources - doctors treating opioid addicts, or enforcement officials (police and Customs) detecting drug offences and seizing the drugs involved. In either case, both the absolute numbers and (perhaps to a lesser extent) any trends in the statistics reflect the effort and resources these services devote to drugs, and the relative 'detectability' of the activity, as much as they reflect the real level of addiction, drug offences, or drug smuggling.

Notifications of Opioid Addiction

Any doctor who 'attends' a patient whom they suspect, or know, to be addicted to certain drugs, must 'notify' the Home Office. These 'notifiable' drugs are a list of thirteen opioids (including heroin, methadone, opium, dipipanone), plus cocaine. But the inclusion of cocaine is a historical legacy of little current significance. For practical purposes, these statistics are to do with opioid addiction - ie, addiction to drugs derived from the opium poppy, or to synthetic drugs with similar properties.

Only confirmed (rather than merely suspected) cases of opioid addiction are counted in the statistics. So in practice, these record the numbers of opioid addicts whose addiction has been confirmed by doctors and notified to the Home Office. Non-addicted opioid use is not counted, nor is addiction to drugs other than opioids. Even addiction itself will not be recorded unless that addict sees a doctor, who recognises their addiction, is reasonably sure of their diagnosis, and knows they must notify the fact to the Home Office.

The Tables

Further difficulties in interpretation arise from the unusual way in which the statistics are presented. *Table 1* gives the key figures. Line 1 shows addicts continuing in treatment from the previous year, line 2, addicts notified during the year who were not previously known to the Home Office; line 3, previously notified addicts who have been re-notified after a break. Adding these together gives (line 4) the total number of addicts known to the Home Office in that year - the so-called 'full year' total.

By the end of the year many of these addicts will no longer be receiving prescriptions for notifiable drugs, and are therefore (for the purposes of the statistics) no longer recorded as addicts (line 5). This may be simply because they have died or because they have been sent to prison, where all addicts are withdrawn from opioids. But 8 out of 10 are dropped from the statistics for unspecified reasons. This could include a multiplicity of outcomes in addition to 'cure', including addicts who have decided to 'go it alone', addicts not accepted for treatment and perhaps some continuing in treatment but not receiving prescriptions for notifiable drugs.

What is left (line 6) are the addicts notified that year who were still receiving prescriptions for notifiable drugs on the last day of the year, a figure which can be thought of as an estimate of the addicts in treatment on any given day. This 'end of year' total is the one usually quoted by the Home Office. Others feel the full year total is more representative; presumably they believe that most of the people who drop out during the year are nevertheless more realistically thought of as continuing to be 'addicts' - even if some are temporarily out of circulation or in remission.

Table 2 gives the age and sex of the addicts known to the Home Office in that year. *Table 3* gives the same breakdown for addicts notified for the first time in that year (sometimes called 'new' addicts, these patients may nevertheless have been addicted for several years before being notified). *Table 4* outlines the drugs being used by these 'new' addicts, and by addicts re-notified after a break in treatment, at the time of their notification. This last point is particularly significant. Once an addict is in treatment, the drugs they are recorded as using are the drugs prescribed for them by their doctor, which may well differ from those they had previously obtained: but drugs recorded at the time of notification will more often have been obtained from non-medical sources, so the breakdown in table 4 relates to the availability of drugs on the illicit market.

Interpretation

Drug abuse indicators studies done in London and Newcastle in the first years of the '80s suggest that the total number of opioid dependents may now be five

TABLE 1

Narcotic drug addicts known to the Home Office - by new notifications and numbers no longer recorded as addicts, UK, 1974-83

NUMBER OF PERSONS

	1974	1975	1976	1977	1978	1979	1980	1981	1982	1983
1. Addicts known to be receiving drugs at 1st January (= line 6 of previous year)	1816	1967	1949	1874	2016	2402	2666	2846	3844	4371
Persons notified during the year as addicts by medical practitioners:[1]										
2. Not previously known[2]	870	922	984	1109	1347	1597	1600	2248	2793	4186
3. Known in earlier years	566	536	541	622	753	788	841	1063	1325	1678
4. TOTAL NUMBER OF ADDICTS KNOWN[3] (= 1 + 2 + 3)	3252	3425	3474	3605	4116	4787	5107	6157	7962	10235
5. Number of persons no longer recorded at 31 December	1285	1476	1600	1589	1714	2121	2261	2313	3591	5156
6. ADDICTS KNOWN TO BE RECEIVING DRUGS AS AT 31 DECEMBER (= 4 - 5)	1967	1949	1874	2016	2402	2666	2846	3844	4371	5079

1. Further details in table 4
2. Further details in table 3
3. Further details in table 2

Source: Home Office Statistical Bulletin, 15 August 1984

TABLE 2

Narcotic drug addicts known to the Home Office - by age and sex, UK, 1974 - 1983

NUMBER OF PERSONS

Age	1974	1975	1976	1977	1978	1979	1980	1981	1982	1983
Under 21	517	377	269	271	289	308	365	478	698	1135
21-24	1215	1177	1056	921	982	1054	995	1161	1536	2042
25-29	874	1123	1311	1399	1628	1843	1882	2110	2569	2977
30-34	206	265	340	414	614	854	1115	1538	2049	2518
35-49	189	229	242	282	313	406	421	503	710	1023
50+	238	221	230	232	242	268	238	248	249	305
Not recorded	13	33	26	86	48	54	91	119	151	235
All ages:										
Females	741	796	828	890	1054	1281	1398	1703	2220	2863
Males	2511	2629	2646	2715	3062	3506	3709	4454	5742	7372
TOTAL:	3252	3425	3474	3605	4116	4787	5107	6157	7962	10235

Source: Calculated from Home Office Statistical Bulletin, 15 August 1984

TABLE 3

Narcotic drug addicts not previously known to the Home Office
notified during the year - by age and sex, UK, 1974-1983

NUMBER OF PERSONS

Age	1974	1975	1976	1977	1978	1979	1980	1981	1982	1983
Under 21	281	192	162	184	207	206	257	357	489	879
21-24	310	351	354	353	432	486	459	644	768	1150
25-29	146	232	306	305	420	516	504	697	826	1081
30-34	39	46	70	96	141	186	213	353	436	590
35-49	29	46	45	59	74	101	74	96	159	251
50+	53	24	32	36	39	59	27	29	28	56
Not recorded	12	31	15	76	34	43	66	72	87	179
All ages:										
Females	205	203	239	292	344	435	460	641	817	1207
Males	665	719	745	817	1003	1162	1140	1607	1976	2979
TOTAL:	870	922	984	1109	1347	1597	1600	2248	2793	4186

Source: Home Office Statistical Bulletin, 15 August 1984

TABLE 4

Narcotic drug addicts notified to the Home Office during the
year by type of drug to which addiction was reported, UK, 1974-1983

NUMBER OF PERSONS

Age	1974	1975	1976	1977	1978	1979	1980	1981	1982	1983
Heroin	840	812	912	957	1269	1559	1657	2334	3006	4786
Methadone	358	345	311	364	366	385	354	436	468	526
Dipipanone	41	109	109	199	241	250	291	390	493	351
Other drugs	197	192	193	211	224	191	139	151	151	201
TOTAL	1436	1458	1525	1731	2100	2385	2441	3311	4118	5864

Addicts taking more than one drug are shown only once in the table under the 'principal' drug of addiction. The order
of priority for determining the principal drug is: 1. Heroin, 2. Methadone, 3. Dipipanone, 4. Other drugs.

Source: Calculated from Home Office Statistical Bulletin, 15 August 1984.

times the number of addicts notified to the Home Office. In any event the consensus of all the available statistics, including seizures (see below), is that illicit opioid use has increased substantially since the late '70s, and that the greatest increase has been in the use of illicitly imported heroin.

This last point is reflected in the increasing proportion (rising from 55% in 1977 to over 80% in 1982) and numbers of addicts notified during the year who were notified as addicted to heroin; prescribing restrictions and policies have ensured that very little of the drug is diverted from legitimate sources, so the majority of these addicts must have been using illicitly imported heroin (see table 4).

Since 1979 there has been an increase in the proportion of 'new' addicts aged under 21, but the figure of 22% for 1983 is still below the proportion under 21 in the early '70s (see table 3).

Enforcement Statistics

Enforcement statistics on drug misuse record the fruits (convictions and drug seizures) of police or Customs action taken against people who have committed offences involving drugs controlled under the Misuse of Drugs Act. The drugs concerned include all those (opioids and cocaine) to which addiction must be notified, together with drugs such as cannabis, LSD, methaqualone, etc. Although more wide ranging than the addiction statistics, there are some notable gaps. In particular barbiturates will not be controlled under the Act until 1985, and therefore do not figure in these statistics.

The Tables

Table 5 lists some of the drugs controlled under the Misuse of Drugs Act, and specifies for each year how many people were found guilty of (or cautioned for - this is relatively rare) offences involving these drugs. Someone may be found guilty of offences involving several drugs. In this case their convictions are reported under each of the drugs, but only once in the total for 'all drugs'. For this reason the figures for the separate drugs may not add up to the total. Table 6 details the ages of these offenders.

The great majority of offenders (94% in 1983) are convicted under the Misuse of Drugs Act. Unlawful possession is by far the most common conviction, involving (in 1983) nearly 90% of all drugs offenders.

TABLE 5

Persons[1] found guilty of or cautioned for drug offences[2] - by type of drug, UK, 1974 - 1983

NUMBER OF PERSONS

Type of Drug	1974	1975	1976	1977	1978	1979	1980	1981	1982	1983
All drugs	12532	11846	12754	12907	13604	14339	17158	17921	20319	23341
Cocaine	375	379	327	309	348	331	476	566	426	563
Heroin	444	393	464	393	483	520	751	808	966	1508
Methadone	464	484	416	347	369	298	363	445	404	379
Dipapanone	369	409	361	378	493	453	440	498	566	370
LSD	905	826	647	279	291	208	246	345	466	451
Cannabis	9517	8987	9946	10607	11572	12409	14910	15388	17410	19966
Amphetamines	1482	1501	1909	1788	1093	760	827	1074	1521	2008
Other drugs	1654	1642	1293	1298	1262	1165	1292	1141	1008	946

1. As the same person may be found guilty of or cautioned for offences involving more than one drug, rows cannot be added together to produce totals.

2. Includes offences under drugs legislation and other offences where drugs were also involved.

Source: Home Office Statistical Bulletin, 15 August 1984

25

TABLE 6

Persons found guilty of or cautioned for drug offences[1] – by age,
UK, 1974 – 1983

NUMBER OF PERSONS

Age	1974	1975	1976	1977	1978	1979	1980	1981	1982	1983
Under 17	335	203	171	185	149	214	282	293	459	588
17–20	4446	3470	3273	3044	3163	3185	3691	4068	5004	6058
21–24	4410	4416	4564	4354	4364	4319	4846	4886	5560	6205
25–29	2129	2441	3168	3442	3674	3952	4665	4709	4808	5150
30+	1212	1316	1578	1882	2254	2669	3674	3965	4488	5340
ALL AGES	12532	11846	12754	12907	13604	14339	17158	17921	20319	23341

1. Includes offences under drugs legislation and other offences where drugs were also involved.

Source: Home Office Statistical Bulletin, 15 August 1984

Table 7 details the quantity of drugs seized by the UK authorities. Figures on the left give the total seized by police *and* by Customs and Excise; figures on the right are quantities seized *only* by Customs and Excise. Customs and Excise officers generally intercept drugs in the process of being illegally imported into Britain. Police seize drugs that have already entered Britain, or those which find their way onto the illicit market from sources internal to the UK, either by diversion from medical supplies or from home-based illicit production.

No great significance should be attached to unusually high or low totals in any one year, as individual seizures of very large amounts can cause unrepresentative fluctuations.

Table 8 gives the numbers of seizures made by the police (as opposed to the quantities seized). About 90% of these seizures will have involved generally small amounts of drugs seized from people in the street or on private premises.

Interpretation

There are no published studies to help estimate what proportion of all drug users are convicted, or what proportion of drugs smuggled into the country are seized. And unlike say robbery or assault, there are no statistics on the number of offences reported to the police which have not resulted in a seizure or a conviction; drug suppliers and users will not generally report offences in which they themselves are implicated and from which they feel themselves to have gained some benefit. This problem is common to other forms of 'victimless' crime, and means that the statistics depend very much on an unknown clear-up rate for drugs offences and seizures. In turn this depends partly on the resources, skill and effort devoted to discovering and prosecuting these activities and the relative detectability of the offence.

In the event, the clear-up rate for drug offences must be very small; for example, it is probable that at least a million people in the UK use cannabis in a year, but less than 20,000 are apprehended, meaning that less than 2% of cannabis offenders are convicted. Cannabis alone accounts for at least 73% of all drug convictions. The clear-up rate for other drugs may differ, but overall the clear-up rate for drugs offences is likely to be around 1-2%.

Customs sometimes guess that they seize 10% of drugs entering the country, but this figure has no scientific basis. More credence can be attached to the fact that since 1978 the proportion of heroin seized which was destined for UK consumption has risen from 10-20% to 80-90%, indicating that the UK is now a

TABLE 7

Quantity of controlled drugs seized and quantity seized by
Customs and Excise – by drug type, UK, 1975-1983

Drug Type	1975		1976		1977		1978		1979	
Class 'A' drugs[1]										
Cocaine	7.1	6.3	9.9	9.4	13.7	12.0	16.1	14.6	24.0	21.6
Dextromoramide	0.017	--	0.019	0.001	0.025	--	0.033	--	0.033	0.005
Dipipanone	0.012	--	0.006	--	0.046	--	0.019	--	0.026	--
Heroin	6.9	4.2	20.2	16.0	26.6	24.0	60.8	58.6	44.9	43.3
Methadone	0.075	--	0.036	--	0.532	--	0.038	--	0.359	0.001
Morphine	7.4	2.3	1.4	0.7	2.0	0.9	3.9	3.1	4.4	2.9
Opium	19.3	7.1	2.7	2.2	18.5	16.0	20.4	10.0	63.2	58.7
Pethidine	0.9	--	0.6	--	2.6	2.0	0.9	0.4	0.6	--
LSD	0.041	--	0.016	0.001	1.488	--	0.007	0.001	0.343	0.241
Other Class A drugs	0.8	0.1	0.8	--	1.2	0.4	0.7	0.4	0.2	0.1
Class 'B' Drugs[1]										
Cannabis herbal	3111	2735	3169	2915	1945	1729	3162	3005	6445	6300
Cannabis plants[2]	5298	--	9718	--	10580	--	8467	--	22306	--
Cannabis resin	2112	1645	1923	1652	2379	2069	3480	3189	5455	5248
Cannabis liquid	84.6	84.3	67.8	41.4	28.5	25.1	55.2	55.0	41.4	39.5
Amphetamine)										
Dexamphetamine)	20.2	0.9	7.6	1.0	18.4	10.8	1.7	0.1	3.9	0.1
Levamphetamine)										
Methylamphetamine	1.2	0.5	0.8	0.5	17.2	13.7	0.3	0.1	4.7	--
Other Class 'B' drugs	3.9	--	0.5	--	0.2	0.1	0.3	0.2	0.2	0.1
Class 'C' Drugs[1]										
Methaqualone	8.5	5.3	1.9	0.4	6.3	4.0	3.2	0.7	3.5	0.2
Other Class 'C' drugs	0.008	0.001	0.014	0.001	0.013	0.002	0.021	0.002	0.051	0.033

1. Refers to the classification of drugs under the Misuse of Drugs Act. 'Class A' Drugs attract the severest maximum penalties, 'Class C' the least severe.

Quantity of controlled drugs seized and quantity seized by
Customs and Excise – by drug type, UK, 1975–1983

Drug Type	1980		1981		1982		1983	
Class 'A' drugs[1]								
Cocaine	40.2	36.0	21.1	15.7	18.8	12.1	95.7	89.7
Dextromoramide	0.028	--	0.022	--	0.027	--	0.011	--
Dipipanone	0.010	--	0.011	--	0.008	--	0.011	--
Heroin	38.2	36.4	93.4	85.8	195.5	185.1	247.1	226.6
Methadone	0.051	0.004	0.953	0.001	0.062	0.001	0.184	--
Morphine	8.0	6.6	6.5	5.2	2.0	1.7	4.6	1.5
Opium	36.2	30.3	16.5	9.3	21.5	17.2	7.8	1.8
Pethidine	0.5	--	0.3	--	0.2	--	0.4	--
LSD	0.005	0.002	0.024	0.011	0.091	0.005	0.024	0.019
Other Class A drugs	1.1	1.0	0.6	0.4	1.6	0.1	0.4	0.2
Class 'B' Drugs[1]								
Cannabis herbal	18419	17943	16874	16627	12996	12576	13735	13453
Cannabis plants[2]	34654	--	21178	3	18091	5	15714	2
Cannabis resin	7753	7440	7818	7517	4413	4003	6817	6470
Cannabis liquid	128.0	120.7	81.6	73.8	34.4	31.8	42.9	16.8
Amphetamine)								
Dexamphetamine)	5.1	0.2	18.0	7.3	12.5	2.2	34.9	12.3
Levamphetamine)								
Methylamphetamine	0.1	--	0.1	--	1.1	--	0.001	--
Other Class 'B' drugs	0.2	0.1	0.2	0.1	0.9	0.2	0.039	--
Class 'C' Drugs[1]								
Methaqualone	3.3	1.3	1.2	0.4	13.0	12.8	3.9	3.8
Other Class 'C' drugs	0.014	0.001	0.005	0.001	0.030	--	0.010	--

2. Number of plants seized

Sources: (i) Total seizures, Home Office Statistical Bulletin, 15 August, 1984.
(ii) Customs and Excise seizures, Statistics of the Misuse of Drugs United Kingdom; Supplementary Tables 1983. Home Office.

TABLE 8

Number of seizures[1] by the Police of controlled drugs –
by drug type, UK, 1974–1983

NUMBER OF SEIZURES

Age	1974	1975	1976	1977	1978	1979	1980	1981	1982	1983
All controlled drugs	9893	9304	10105	11305	11619	13913	14946	16667	19014	22745
Class 'A' drugs[2]										
Cocaine	197	170	186	167	197	293	365	396	314	558
Dextromoramide	50	59	53	60	55	78	86	80	77	51
Dipipanone	150	192	158	240	282	349	259	368	428	292
Heroin	302	221	304	216	285	515	612	731	848	1745
Methadone	301	258	247	210	232	287	317	396	354	411
Morphine	291	276	220	290	244	275	253	204	177	138
Opium	117	166	97	82	65	114	102	98	68	68
Pethidine	156	146	138	151	135	153	158	123	95	64
LSD	590	613	425	191	273	200	243	356	430	474
Other Class A drugs	207	156	141	224	130	89	102	107	133	90
Class 'B' drugs[2]										
Cannabis herbal	3401	3024	2822	2342	2845	4251	7201	6765	7077	6591
Cannabis plants	325	436	628	872	819	1324	2351	1786	1707	1294
Cannabis resin	4840	4612	5655	7507	7739	8303	6216	8131	9986	13231
Cannabis liquid	72	163	102	86	59	160	188	206	246	264
Amphetamine)										
Dexamphetamine)	806	862	1224	909	570	615	645	1036	1605	2283
Levamphetamine)										
Methylamphetamine	40	196	189	425	85	117	76	43	10	7
Other Class B drugs	229	245	183	214	214	257	198	220	244	191

31

TABLE 8 (Continued)

**Number of seizures[1] by the Police of controlled drugs –
by drug type, UK, 1974-1983**

Age	NUMBER OF SEIZURES									
	1974	1975	1976	1977	1978	1979	1980	1981	1982	1983
Class 'C' drugs[2]										
Methaqualone	543	378	282	314	286	322	271	116	47	28
Other Class C drugs	12	11	9	7	5	8	18	9	4	6

1. As the same seizure can involve more than one drug type, rows cannot be added together to produce totals or
   subtotals.
2. Refers to classification under the Misuse of Drugs Act. Class 'A' drugs attract the severest maximum penalties,
   Class 'C' the least severe.
Source: Statistics of the misuse of drugs United Kingdom: supplementary tables 1983. Home Office.

recognised market for illicit heroin, rather than just a staging-post to other countries where the drug is in greater demand.

The pattern of Customs v. police seizures in table 7 indicates that increasing quantities of heroin and cocaine are being imported into Britain, and that substantial quantities of cannabis continue to be imported at the same time as home cultivation (indicated by number of plants seized) continues to flourish. UK-based production of amphetamine sulphate (which appears to be increasing) and of LSD probably accounts for the relatively large quantities of these drugs seized by the police.

Trends in numbers of police seizures (table 8) reflect trends in 'street' availability and use of controlled drugs. These confirm observations of an increase in the use of heroin, cocaine and the amphetamines since the late '70s, but also confirm that cannabis continues to dominate the illicit drug market. Seizure statistics indicate that in the '80s illicitly imported heroin has displaced opioids diverted from medical supplies as the major feature of the illicit market in opioid drugs; from a low of 17% in 1977 the percentage of heroin seizures has increased each year to represent 63% of all opioid seizures in 1983.

Solvents

Although not a controlled drug, in recent years the police in Scotland have published statistics of the number of solvent misusers coming to their attention. The figure was 2,399 in 1980, 3,312 in 1981, and 2,168 in 1982. With the change in the law in Scotland from July 1983, making solvent misuse grounds for referral to a children's hearing, further statistics may become available in the annual Statistical Bulletin on Children's Hearing Statistics issued by the Scottish Education Department and available from the Scottish Office Library (tel. 031-556-8400 for further details). Corresponding statistics are not available for the remainder of the UK.

APPROVED RECREATIONAL USE OF DRUGS

There is a wide range of drugs affecting the mind whose medical use is socially acceptable. But there are very few drugs whose non-medical use is (generally speaking) socially acceptable, and not subject to blanket legal prohibition. In the UK, alcoholic drinks, tobacco, and caffeine-containing beverages (tea, coffee and soft drinks) are the main substances involved.

Alcohol

Statistics on alcohol use are far more detailed than statistics on drug misuse. They show that in Great Britain in 1982 just 1 in 16 men and 1 in 8 women of 'drinking age' (18-plus) are virtual abstainers. the rest, well over 90% of the adult population, drink to a greater or lesser extent. On average the UK population aged 15 and over drinks the equivalent of just over a pint of beer a day.

Men drinkers consume the equivalent of one and a half pints of beer a day, women about half a pint. About 40% of both men and women are classified as 'frequent light' drinkers (typically drinking no more than the equivalent of two pints of beer at a time, but drinking at least once a week), and this is the most common pattern of drinking. Just 1% of women, but 1 in 5 men, are 'heavier' drinkers (three and a half to four pints or more at least once a week).

About 6% of men and 1% of women consistently exceed the levels of alcohol consumption generally considered to cause serious risk of physical damage (three and a half pints/day for men, two and a half pints for women). It has been estimated that at least 300,000 people in the UK and perhaps as many as 740,000 suffer from severe drink-related problems.

Getting drunk is a relatively common event. On their own admission, nearly half the male population and one in seven of women will have been drunk in the last three months. Younger adults drink more. In the late teens and early twenties, alcohol consumption is 40-50% above average, and along with this goes a higher incidence of being drunk and of heavier drinking, the latter reaching a maximum of 35% amongst young men aged 18-24. In the 13-16 years age range, about a third of children drink at least once a week, but mostly in the home and generally small amounts.

Proportionately, heavier drinking is over twice as common among male manual workers (27%) as among male non-manual workers (11%).

Consumption of all kinds of alcoholic beverages has been increasing. Since the early '50s there has been a 74% increase in the average consumption of alcoholic drinks amongst the UK population aged 15+, a trend which may be related to the fact that, relative to wages, the 'price of a pint' decreased by half over the same period. On top of this, since 1974 there has been an expansion in the 'home-brew' market for beers, wines and cider. In 1981, some 2 million people in the UK brewed nearly 300 million pints of beer in their own homes.

Tobacco

The extent of tobacco smoking is also relatively well documented. A survey in 1982 indicated that in Great Britan about 39% of people aged 16 or over smoked cigarettes or cigars. The percentage was higher for men than for women (45 v 34%), but below retirement age the percentage of women cigarette smokers is only a few per cent below the figure for men, and there is practically no sex difference in the prevalence of cigarette smoking amongst schoolchildren. Male cigarette smokers consume on average 17 a day, women 14 a day.

Smoking is most prevalent of all amongst male manual workers; nearly half of all unskilled and semi-skilled men workers smoke as against 20-30% of men in non-manual occupations.

Just under a fifth of all men and over 1 in 10 of all women smoke sufficiently (20 plus cigarettes every day) to be classified as heavy smokers. Heavy smoking is most common amongst male manual workers (around 1 in 5) and least common amongst male and female professional workers (1 in 10 and 1 in 20 respectively).

Whilst 1 in 5 eleven year olds have tried smoking, practically 0% regularly smoke one or more cigarettes a week. By thirteen years of age the prevalence of regular smoking rises to 8-9%, and by fifteen, to over a quarter. Of those youngsters that do smoke, the majority consume ten or more cigarettes a week.

About 30% of 16-19 year olds smoke, each smoker consuming an average of 11-12 cigarettes a day. From 20 to 60 years of age the prevalence of smoking is more or less constant at around 40%, decreasing to 33% for men and 23% for women aged 60 or more.

The percentage of the population who smoke has decreased since the early '50s, when 60% of men and 40% of women smoked manufactured cigarettes. However, until recently each smoker was smoking more, with the result that the total number of cigarettes smoked each year was increasing. This trend has been reversed since the mid '70s, with each smoker's average cigarette consumption falling slightly (due almost entirely to the decrease in male smokers' average consumption) and the total number of cigarettes smoked falling from a peak of over 137,000 million in 1973 to 102,000 million in 1982.

Since the 1950s there has been a switch to filtered cigarettes, and since the '60s the tar, nicotine and carbon monoxide yields of most brands sold in the UK has declined.

Caffeine

Caffeine-containing beverages are consumed largely for taste or relaxation, and as a social activity, without much conscious interest in their drug content. But caffeine is potentially a quite powerful stimulant.

In medical usage, 200mg is the standard stimulant dose. Compared with this, each small cup of brewed coffee provides from 40-280mg of caffeine (average 115mg drip method, 80mg percolated), instant coffee from 30-120mg (average 65m), tea from 25-110mg (average 60mg), and a bottle or can of soft drink from 30-46mg. About 70% of all UK adults drink coffee, 86% drink tea. In Britain daily per-capita consumption of tea averages just over four cups, and of instant coffee, over two cups.

Caffeine is also an ingredient in some of the most well-known brands of proprietary analgesics available in the UK. As we will see later (part 4, 'Over-the-counter medicines') over a million people take these kinds of pills every day. With up to 50mg in each tablet, it would be easy for someone using the caffeine-containing products to add as much again to their caffeine consumption from beverages.

Average daily UK caffeine consumption from all sources has been estimated at over 440mg per person.

MEDICAL DRUG USE

The medical use of psychotropic drugs is controlled by the Medicines Act (as well as, for some drugs, by the Misuse of Drugs Act). Most full-strength psychotropics are only available on prescription from a doctor, so there is some check on their being used inappropriately. Less powerful mind-altering drugs, like aspirin or paracetamol, and very dilute mixtures, such as cough syrups containing opiates, can be bought over-the-counter from a pharmacy only, or from any shop.

Prescribed Psychotropics

Conventional medical use of drugs is not generally thought of as 'drugtaking'. But 'leakage' (or diversion) from the legitimate production, distribution and medical use of drugs, has been an important supply route for the illicit market. This was seen most dramatically in the '60s when excess heroin, legitimately prescribed by doctors to heroin addicts, was passed on to other people, and was the direct cause of a very rapid increase in heroin addiction. The same kind of thing happens today, not so much with heroin, but with other opioids and with drugs like barbiturates. Thefts from pharmacies, warehouses and doctors' surgeries, are another important source for the illicit market in drugs.

Also a certain proportion of the people being prescribed drugs on a long-term basis will be using them for the same kinds of reasons that addicts use heroin or barbiturates - not because they any longer alleviate the original complaint, but because they have come to need the drug for itself. No one really knows how big this proportion might be.

Prescription Statistics

Table 9 reproduces official statistics on the number of prescriptions for psychotropic drugs issued by general practitioners. It first gives the total of prescriptions issued; then the total number of prescriptions of preparations which affect the nervous system; and then breaks down this last category according to the 'therapeutic class' of the drug involved. One complication arises from the fact that a drug of a given chemical type may be prescribed for different therapeutic purposes, so the headings in this table cannot be translated into headings which relate to the actual substance prescribed. For instance, benzodiazepines may be prescribed as tranquillisers, as hypnotics, or as anti-convulsants, so benzodiazepine prescriptions might be counted under any of these categories in the table.

However, it is known that in 1981 doctors in Great Britain issued nearly 28,850,000 prescriptions for benzodiazepines, making these the most frequently prescribed drugs in Britain. The great majority of these prescriptions are to help patients cope with anxiety or insomnia.

Surveys

There are also several survey-type studies of prescription-drug usage. One such study in 1977 suggested that 12% of the adult population of England and Wales had taken a prescribed psychotropic drug in the previous fortnight, and that some 7% had first been prescribed that drug a year or more ago. Long-term use of prescribed psychotropics is far more common amongst the elderly, with 14% of those aged 55 or more taking drugs first prescribed a year or more ago, as opposed to 3% of those aged 18-54. Peak usage was found amongst middle-class, elderly women, of whom 1 in 6 were being prescribed psychotropics on a long-term basis.

TABLE 9

Family practitioner pharmaceutical services. Total number of prescriptions and number of prescriptions of preparations acting on the nervous system
- by therapeutic class, Great Britain, 1976-1982

Therapeutic class	THOUSANDS OF PRESCRIPTIONS						
	1976	1977	1978	1979	1980	1981	1982
ALL CLASSES	348490	351331	365497	362483	361274	357273	370275
PREPARATIONS ACTING ON THE NERVOUS SYSTEM	88183	89072	91111	88019	84153	82581	83789
General anaesthetics	1	--	--	--	1	1	--
Hypnotics	16715	16967	17212	17460	16546	16605	16862
Sedatives and tranquillisers	25007	24816	25043	24390	22493	21920	21413
Anticonvulsants	4093	4051	4156	4049	4222	4313	4230
Anti-parkinsonism drugs	1379	1476	1517	1555	1638	1657	1727
Analgesics major	4116	4271	4286	4310	4277	4466	4933
Analgesics minor	20014	21005	22877	20996	20864	19822	21046
Local anaesthetics and counter-irritants	2670	2659	2545	2375	2092	1903	1992
Neuro-muscular blocking agents	--	--	--	--	--	--	--
Other muscle relaxants	316	291	306	323	336	295	304
CNS stimulants	2462	2564	2334	2127	1970	1806	1718
CNS stimulants and depressant combinations	129	109	105	28	8	2	1
Anti-depressants	8067	7759	7812	7582	7241	7539	7468
Anti-depressants and sedative/tranquilliser combinations	1745	1680	1582	1493	1368	1259	1134
Anti-emetics	1070	1044	1063	1070	864	775	771
Appetite suppressants (non CNS stimulants)	359	287	232	218	180	164	142
Other preparations	42	41	41	44	55	54	50

Source: Personal communication from the DHSS Statistics and Research Division, Russell Square, London

37

An earlier (1971) study found that 1 in 7 of the adult UK population had taken a tranquilliser or sedative in the past year, and that over 8% of the population had been taking them every day for at least a month.

The proportion of women making short or long-term use of prescribed psychotropics is consistently found to be about double the proportion of men, though this sex difference appears to even out among the elderly. There is evidence from a 'Marplan' survey that a third of all women have at some time been prescribed tranquillisers, over a quarter sleeping pills, and that very nearly half (46%) the women in Britain have been prescribed one or the other at some time in their life. This same survey found that about a fifth of the women ever prescribed these drugs were taking them at least three times a week.

A different, and perhaps rather more reliable, survey in Scotland showed that over a quarter of all the women in the sample had ever taken psychotropic medicines (sleeping pills, anti-depressants or tranquillisers) on a regular basis; at the time of the survey, 1 in 7 women were taking these drugs on a regular basis, about evenly split between sleeping pills and tranquillisers, with a much smaller percentage (2% of the total) also taking anti-depressants.

Whilst the majority of tranquillisers are prescribed for anxiety or sleeping problems, in a large proportion of patients these problems are associated with physical disorders.

There is research evidence that tranquillisers lose their therapeutic effectiveness after 4 months continuous use, so the widespread long-term use of these drugs has been taken to reflect reliance on tranquillisers to cope with life's problems, or dependence. The incidence of withdrawal symptoms on discontinuing tranquillisers is some indication of the risk of physical dependence. The most relevant study to date found that nearly half of a small group of patients taking tranquillisers in normal doses for an average of several years experienced withdrawal symptoms when the dosage was gradually reduced.

Over-The-Counter Medicines

Information on the extent of usage of non-prescription medicines is less readily available. But survey studies in the early '70s found that 9% of the British population used minor analgesics (aspirin, paracetamol, etc) weekly, and nearly 3% (over a million people) use them every day. Analgesic self- medication is consistently reported to be most prevalent amongst young women.

A SYNTHESIS

The age, incompleteness, and unreliability of most research and statistical information of the extent of drug misuse, means that an up-to-date and more realistic assessment can only be made by complementing these with the impressions of people working in the field. So where this conclusion strays beyond the research and official statistics already quoted, its assertions should be taken as no more than (more or less) informed guesswork.

Drug Misuse

It is thought that some 5 million people in the UK have taken cannabis, with at least a million taking the drug in a year. Most people who take cannabis are between 20 and 35 years of age. In a few youth subcultures (eg, social science students at university), almost as many people will have taken cannabis as those who have not, but in other parts of the population (eg, elderly people), cannabis smoking will be practically unknown. Overall, the increase in the prevalence of cannabis use has probably levelled off somewhat since a rapid rise in the early '70s, but it remains by far the most popular of the drugs controlled under the Misuse of Drugs Act. Compared to the '60s, cannabis is used by a wider range of people rather than being relatively limited to young non-conformist groups, such as the '60s 'hippies'.

Of these 'controlled' drugs, amphetamines come next, a long way behind cannabis. From time to time there are reports of amphetamine use being prevalent amongst groups of youngsters who attend late-night dance venues, much as happened in the '60s, but amphetamines are also used intermittently to help maintain long periods of concentration or physical effort amongst students and in certain occupations.

The available surveys show that vanishingly small proportions of the population have ever used heroin or other opioid drugs, though there is evidence of a quite rapid increase since the late '70s. There are reports of heroin smoking becoming quite common amongst older teenagers in certain inner-city areas, such as in Glasgow and London. Increased and more widespread use of heroin is often linked to its increased availability, decreased cost (relative to wages, the price of heroin on the illicit market has halved since 1978), and rising unemployment. During 1983 there were probably at least 50,000 heavy users of opiates in the UK, though at any one time the figure would have been lower, say 25-30,000. Some workers guess that as many again used opiates on a more occasional basis. Most of the occasional users who are using illicit heroin will be sniffing or smoking the drug as opposed to injecting. Nevertheless these estimates imply that less than 0.5% of the UK population misuse opioid drugs in any given year. Whilst increased heroin use amongst the young working class has captured the headlines, it is likely that heroin use has increased across all social classes and most age groups.

LSD was widely used in the late '60s and early '70s. Enforcement statistics suggest a decline in usage since that time, though in recent years there may have been some recovery. However, it is likely that less than 1% of the population will have experienced LSD.

Cocaine use is relatively rare, though the drug has gained in popularity since the mid '70s. Due largely to its expense, cocaine sniffing on anything than an occasional basis will be rare, except in some well-off 'fashionable' groups. However, occasional use has become quite common amongst drug using circles.

In 1979 it was estimated that dependence on barbiturates was as widespread as opioid dependence. In addition, it was known that many opioid dependents used these two types of drugs interchangeably, depending on availability, as alternative routes to the desired state of sedation. Barbiturates misuse seems to have declined during the '80s, both as the drug has become less available on prescription, and as heroin has become more available. Nevertheless, the number of people experiencing problems due to their misuse of non-opioid drugs in general (barbiturates and others) is still thought to be at least as great as the number of opioid dependents.

The eating of hallucinogenic mushrooms has been reported as a common event in urban conurbations in Britain, and in rural Wales. A number of these mushrooms grow wild in the UK, but the most common, and the most commonly used of them is psilocybe semilanceata (Liberty Cap) containing psilocin and psilocybin. Between 1978 and 1981, enquiries received by the National Poisons Information Service concerning psilocybe intoxication increased considerably, the largest single age group of patients being in their late 'teens. This provides some statistical support for indication that psilocybe use has indeed been increasing in recent years, most visibly amongst groups of teenagers.

Solvents are an exception to the general rule that drugs are used most by people of greater than school age. With these 'drugs', usage is greatest in the 12-17 years age range and more commonly seen in boys than girls. In some areas, quite a high proportion of the local adolescents may try solvent sniffing, but very few will persist once they move beyond the age range where sniffing is 'child's play', to one where it is looked down upon as childish, and alcohol becomes the main drug pre-occupation. However, there are recent indications that a few older people have either continued to use or started to use solvents, due to the relative expense of alcohol.

Overall, school students misuse drugs very infrequently - less than 1 in 10 will have ever tried any of the drugs controlled under the Misuse of Drugs Act, and three-quarters of these will have confined their illegal drug use to cannabis. Drug misuse is most common in the period after leaving school up to the approach of middle age, perhaps because it is (or at least, is thought to be) associated with a relatively unconventional and unsettled life style. Drug misuse of any kind is more common amongst males than amongst females.

Medical and 'Approved' Recreational Drugtaking

The extent of drug misuse is dwarfed by the extent of the non-medical use of 'socially approved' drugs, like alcohol, tobacco and caffeine. Regular consumption of caffeine containing beverages is practically ubiquitous throughout the age range, whilst abstention from alcohol is practised by less than 1 in 10 of the adult population. Compared with 50,000 heavy opioid users, there may be half a million 'problem drinkers'. Nevertheless, the vast majority of drinkers stay within medically 'safe' limits and avoid physical dependence.

Nearly 40% of the adult population smoke tobacco, and nearly half of these are heavy smokers. The prevalence of smoking is high throughout the adult age range, and laws against selling tobacco to the under 16s fail to prevent a quarter of younger adolescents smoking. Tobacco smoking and alcohol drinking are - like drug misuse - more common amongst men, and each man tends to consume more than each woman. However, over the years this sex gap has been diminishing: in particular, there is now relatively little difference between the prevalence and pattern of cigarette smoking in men and women.

This sex-relationship is reversed when it comes to the long or short-term use of prescribed psychotropics, like tranquillisers and sedatives. It is thought that 1 in 7 of British adults take these drugs at some time during the year, and 1 in 40 take them throughout the year, though opinions differ on how much of this is appropriate medical use, and how much arises from a greater or lesser dependency on the drug. On the basis of the available research, it has been suggested that 200,000 UK adults would experience withdrawal symptoms if they tried to stop taking benzodiazepines. It has also been suggested that at least half the patients prescribed benzodiazepine tranquillisers for a year or more are taking the drugs because of dependence rather than because they remain therapeutically effective. However, there are few studies directly relevant to the question of dependence (a compulsion to continue taking a drug) rather than the appearance of withdrawal symptoms (which may or may not result in physical dependence).

FURTHER INFORMATION AND REFERENCES

All the publications referred to are available for reference at ISDD Institute for Study of Drug Dependence, 1-4 Hatton Place, Hatton Garden, London EC1N 8ND. ISDD's library will answer enquiries by letter or telephone.

Drug Misuse Surveys

Two earlier reviews were consulted extensively to compile the first section of this chapter. The first was 'The epidemiology of self-reported drug misuse in the United Kingdom' by Joy Mott (of the Home Office Research Unit), which appeared in the United Nations *Bulletin on Narcotics*, Volume 28 no. 1, in 1976. The second was a chapter by Gerry Stimson called 'Epidemiological research on drug use in general populations', which appeared in the book *Drug Problems in Britain: A Review of Ten Years* edited by G. Edwards and C. Busch, and published by Academic Press in 1981. The third chapter of that book is also a useful explanation and review of trends in notifications statistics.

Copies of the latest surveys on student drug use (*Student culture: 1968-1978*, by J. Crutchley, N. South and J. Young) are available from the authors at Middlesex Polytechnic in London.

The latest survey of drug use amongst schoolchildren (from five schools in the Lothian region of Scotland) which also investigated drug use amongst the same group after leaving school, is due to be published shortly (*Alcohol, drugs and school-leavers*, Plant M.A., Peck D.F., Samuel E. London: Tavistock, 1985).

Drug Misuse Statistics

Full sets of the available statistics on notifications of opioid addiction, drug law convictions, sentencing for drugs offences, and police and Customs seizures of controlled drugs, can be obtained from the Statistical Department, Home Office, Tolworth Tower, Surbiton, Surrey. In recent years they have given the basic statistics in the form of an annual Statistical Bulletin entitled *Statistics of the misuse of drugs in the United Kingdom* supplemented from time to time by a more detailed publication entitled *Statistics of the misuse of drugs United Kingdom: supplementary tables*. The last two issues of these publications were priced at £2.50 and £6.00 respectively, but the reader is advised to telephone the Home Office on 01-399 5191 for details of dates and prices of the latest publications in the series.

Reports on the Misuse of Drugs

Research by the Drug Indicators Project (DIP) into problem drug use in Camden & Islington in North London has been the basis for recent estimates of the overall extent of opioid dependence in the UK. DIP's observations and research findings have been drawn upon heavily in the fifth section of this chapter and have been used to help interpret the official statistics in the second section. At the time of writing their latest published report is in ISDD's 'Druglink' information letter, no. 19, pages 22-24. For a copy send £0.50 to ISDD and ask for a copy of article number 41916.

Alcohol and Tobacco

The annual *General Household Survey* from the Office of Population Censuses and Surveys is the major regular source of survey statistics on alcohol and tobacco use. These surveys are available through HMSO and cover alcohol and tobacco every second year (the figures used in this publication were from the 1982 edition). The publication *Social Trends* gives a digest of the statistics from the general household survey plus figures on trends in overall consumption. Both these regular publications should be available on the reference shelves of large public libraries.

Prescribed Drugs

A mimeographed fact sheet entitled 'Prevalence of psychotropic drugtaking amongst women in the UK' is available from ISDD (price £0.25 plus £0.15 p&p), part B of which reviews the available information on prescribed psychotropics.

The results of the most important recent UK survey on prescribed drugs usage have been described in two articles by Robert Anderson of the Institute for Social Studies in Medical Care. The first, 'Prescribed medicines: who takes what?' was published in 1980 in the *Journal of Epidemiology and Community Health*, vol 34, no. 4. The second, 'The use of repeatedly prescribed medicines', was published, also in 1980, in the *Journal of the Royal College of General Practitioners,* vol. 30, pages 609-613.

Published prescription statistics can be found in the latest edition of the *Health and Personal Social Services Statistics for England* available through HMSO. These give a regional breakdown and also tables on the cost of prescriptions, but are several years behind the latest of the unpublished statistics reproduced in table 9.

N.B. Most of the tables in this publication are available separately from ISDD as a leaflet entitled 'Official statistics on drug-taking in Britain'. The leaflet is intended to be used as a 'handout' at meetings, courses, conferences etc., as part of an overall information 'package'. It is available at £0.15 per copy plus p&p.

This chapter is also available as a separate publication (price £1) from ISDD.

Counselling Problem Drinkers - Research and Practice

Bill Saunders

Research from a variety of sources indicates that primary care workers are not enthusiastic about counselling problem drinkers. In one study in which the attitudes of front-line community based workers were assessed, the respondents reported that they were unsure as to how to counsel problem drinkers, dubious about the legitimacy of their role in counselling such clients and were generally lacking in commitment to this client group[1]. It is therefore a somewhat curious turn of events that in two recent reports on the provision of services for problem drinkers[2][3] the principle recommendation has been that the primary care worker is the ideal professional to respond to the needs of problem drinking clients. In order to understand this paradox it is necessary to consider recent research evidence about the effectiveness of the treatment of problem drinkers and certain research findings about problem drinkers as a client group.

COUNSELLING PROBLEM DRINKERS - SOME RECENT HISTORY

Although alcohol problems are in no way a new phenomenon, treatment responses for excessive drinking are of comparatively recent origin. The development of such services was largely prompted by the report of a World Health Organisation expert sub-committee which first met in 1951 and eventually recommended that alcohol problems could only be reduced if a substantial investment was made in the provision of treatment services[4]. In Britain, this recommendation was accepted by the then Ministry of Health and throughout the 1960s regional alcoholism treatment units (A.T.U.'s) were established. At the same time, a voluntary organisation - the National Council on Alcoholism - was formed with the express remit of setting up local counselling services. In the A.T.U.'s the type of treatment offered reflected developments within general psychiatric practice of that time and there was much enthusiasm for intensive, group psychotherapy based in-patient programmes. Similarly, the local Councils on Alcoholism, whilst not being able to offer in-patient care, based their treatment response on group therapy methods. At this time, in all the treatment agencies the goal of treatment was total abstinence with the philosophy that if abstention was achieved then other aspects of the client's life would inevitably improve.

The creation of new services for problem drinkers resulted in the recruitment of health care professionals who initially relied for their information about alcohol problems on the established wisdom of Alcoholics Anonymous and the associated disease concept of alcoholism. Yet many of these new recruits to alcohol treatment brought with them, along with their counselling ability, the additional talents of curiosity and skill in undertaking research. The dearth of research and the increasing prevalence of alcohol problems ensured that throughout the late 1960s and 1970s alcohol research became of some priority, and alcohol studies as such became a legitimate endeavour.

The problem was, however, that this burgeoning research literature rather than testifying to the conscientious work of many clinicians, was replete with results that challenged the very basis on which much of the treatment was conducted and raised doubts about the value of the treatment provided. As a precis it is possible to note that four interrelated themes can be highlighted from the alcohol treatment literature that was published in the 1970s and taken altogether these issues have had a marked impact upon the treatment of alcohol related problems.

PROBLEMS IN TREATMENT (1) - THE TWO WORLDS OF ALCOHOLISM

The first of these themes is that of the two worlds of alcoholism. This expression, coined by Room (5), reflects the very real differences between those clients who attended treatment agencies and those problem drinkers who are detected in community surveys, but who are at the time of their identification not in treatment. Although something of a caricature the general finding is that the typical community survey identified problem drinker is male, in his mid-thirties, married, employed and with a problem drinking history of less than ten years duration. However, the average patient in clinical samples is usually male, 40-45 years of age, with a disrupted pattern of relationships, poor employment record and often afflicted with an array of medical and psychological disabilities. Such patients normally report a long - in excess of ten years - history of alcohol use and report being dependent on alcohol. One accepted explanation for this discrepancy between epidemiological and clinical samples of problem drinkers is that problem drinkers delay their attendance at helping agencies until considerable social and personal difficulties have accrued. This is important because evidence from the treatment literature clearly shows that factors such as social stability, quality of relationships and work record are of considerable prognostic importance.

PROBLEMS IN TREATMENT (2) - CLIENTS' CHARACTERISTICS

This second theme of clients' characteristics has been highlighted by Costello who, in a series of treatment evaluation reviews[6][7], has shown that clients who at time of presentation have intact marriages, are employed and who are socially stable, fare far better than do clients who come into contact with treatment at a time in their lives when their social resources are depleted. It is possible to summarise the impact of treatment, in terms of improved outcome rates in the following diagram.

The significance of Costello's findings is that this outcome distribution occurs irrespective of the nature of the treatment given. For example the importance of group therapy in the treatment of alcohol related problems has been repeatedly stressed (e.g. see [8]) yet when the type of client is taken into consideration any reported influence of group therapy disappears. In fact Armor, Polich and Stambul[9] in their recent and comprehensive review of alcoholism treatment in America were forced to admit, albeit reluctantly, that:

'It is hard not to conclude that remission and eventual recovery depend to a major extent on the characteristics and behaviour of the individual client rather than on treatment characteristics' (p164).

The treatment problems posed by the 'two worlds of alcoholism' and the associated prognostic influence of clients' characteristics are made more complex by a third issue that is contained within the treatment literature and this concerns the amount or intensity of treatment that clients require.

PROBLEMS IN TREATMENT (3) - 'TREATMENT' OR 'ADVICE'

As may be appreciated, in the early days of the A.T.U.s in Britain the treatment provided was of an intensive and longterm nature. However, the rising prevalence of alcohol problems in the next two decades (which can best be gauged by the figure that between 1952 and 1980 admissions for alcoholism rose from 512 to over 13,000) placed an excessive demand upon the existing in-patient facilities. Thus out-patient and day patient programmes became more commonplace.

48

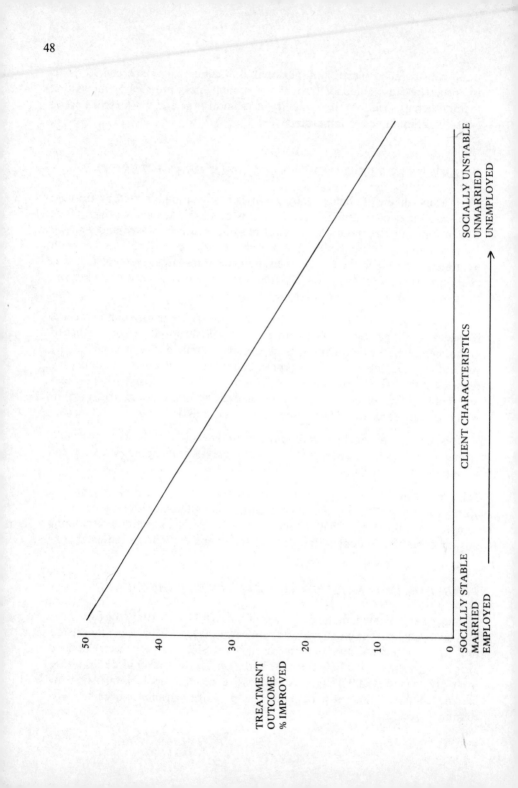

The development of these services resulted in comparative evaluations being undertaken and several studies[10][11] failed to demonstrate the expected superiority of in-patient care over less intensive regimes. Awareness of this feature of 'no-difference' was considerably heightened by the publication of what has become known as the Maudsley Treatment Versus Advice Study[12]. In this study one hundred male problem drinkers who attended the Maudsley Hospital in London were, after a detailed and careful assessment session, randomly allocated to therapy of either a 'treatment' or an 'advice' type. Available to the treatment group was an array of possible services which were deemed to be representative of the type of intervention offered by progressive, good standard A.T.U.s. Thus, dependent upon the individuals' requirements, detoxification, in-patient or out-patient care, group therapy, psychiatric follow up, referral to A.A. and social work support were offered. Those patients allocated to the advice group received a detailed feedback of information from their assessment session and were advised to abstain from alcohol. The only further contact offered was a once a month social work visit but this was restricted to monitoring prognosis only.

Patients in both groups were then followed up at one and two year intervals after their initial treatment contact. As Orford and Edwards[12] note the results were unequivocal. In both the treatment and advice groups remission rates were the same, with approximately one third of each group being improved. The authors also noted that it was not the case that the more severe, and less socially stable clients did better with the more intensive treatment regime and that the advice session was only of sufficient impact to ameliorate the condition of the less chronic patients. However, this latter statement has been criticised and it is possible, within the data presented by Orford and Edwards, to interpret the results as indicating that the more intensive treatment did result in better outcome for the more severe clients. Whatever the truth of this matter it is fair to say that this study has had a major impact upon the alcohol problems treatment field and that there is now little support for intensive intervention.

PROBLEMS IN TREATMENT (4) - THE EFFECTIVENESS OF TREATMENT

Indeed the whole treatment giving industry has been under scrutiny because of the failure of evaluation research to demonstrate clearly that treatment is an effective and potent force in the remission process. A number of recent reviews of the treatment outcome literature do exist of which the best known are by Emrick[13], Clare[14] and Miller and Hester[15]. These reviews collectively cite nearly 1,000 treatment studies published in the period 1950-1980. In their conclusions, each of the authors acknowledge that to date little success in the treatment of alcoholism has been recorded. For example, Emrick[13] was forced to conclude that:

'In a practical sense (alcoholics are) as likely to stop drinking completely for six months or longer when they have no or minimal treatment as when they have more than minimal treatment'(page 98).

Miller and Hester[15] in what is the most recent and undoubtedly the most authoritative review duly noted:

'First of all it is clear that certain treatments are not supported by research to date which has suggested that they are ineffective, uneconomical or unjustifiably hazardous for problem drinkers... The majority of treatment procedures for problem drinkers warrant a 'Scotch Verdict' of unproved at the present time. Ironically the most widely accepted and commonly used treatment techniques currently fall into this category of unproved' (page 108).

However, in spite of their general pessimism about the effectiveness of treatment both Emrick[13] and Miller and Hester[15] conclude their reviews optimistically, though for different reasons. Emrick[13] whilst not being able to find any evidence for the superiority of any one type of therapy did note that there was an association evident between clients being in contact with treatment and being improved. It is necessary to note that this finding does not indicate that treatment works - it is an association between two factors rather than a demonstration of cause and effect. This positive association may reflect either a client characteristic - for example a strong commitment to change and a determination to succeed, or it may reflect non-specific treatment aspects such as the opportunity to mix with other sober people, establish new relationships and pass time without drinking. Whatever the explanation the fact of this correlation between duration of therapy contact and good outcome is important, for it may well be that if strategies that maintain contact with therapy can be found then outcome rates may improve.

Miller and Hester's[15] optimism is based on findings from investigations in which non-abstinence or controlled drinking therapies were evaluated. In a series of experiments conducted by Miller and his colleagues[16][17] various controlled drinking treatments were found to be more effective than either no treatment (being placed on a waiting list) or discussion based therapies. It is necessary to note that the groups of patients used in these investigations were far different from the normal British treatment attender in that they possessed the characteristics of the community detected problem drinkers outlined by Room (5) in his use of the term 'the two worlds of alcoholism'. Furthermore, the average weekly alcohol consumption of clients in Miller's studies did not exceed 50 units of alcohol per week. This total - the approximate equivalent of 25 pints per week - needs to be compared with the weekly average reported in British A.T.U. studies which is of the order of 120-140 units or 60-70 pints per week[18].

However, whilst acknowledging that Miller's patients possessed characteristics likely to be associated with successful outcome the importance of his work is considerable, especially for the following reasons. First his work demonstrates that it is possible to attract into some type of therapeutic contact socially intact and relatively undamaged patients who once in treatment do appear to benefit from the experience. Most interesting, however, is the evidence presented by Miller and Taylor[16] which shows that much of value can be achieved via the use of self-help manuals and very minimal therapist contact. Miller and Taylor report improved outcome rates in excess of 70% and this was achieved by an assessment of the individual's current life and alcohol problems and the 'prescription' of an informative guide about how to drink safely.

In many ways this work epitomises the developing ethos in the alcohol studies field in that the early insight-oriented psychotherapeutic procedures which are complex and costly to provide are being replaced by straightforward, education based activities which are comprehensible to the client and deal with the core problem - his or her drinking behaviour. Thus Miller's self-management guide encourages patients to examine the situations in which excessive drinking is likely to occur and plan relevant coping strategies. Clients generate their own drinking rules and regulations and are provided with case histories which contain hints about techniques likely to be associated with safe (or at least safer) drinking behaviour. The emphasis in this approach is that drinking excessively has far more to do with learning and an interaction between the individual and his environment than any 'within the skin' psychological or biological disorder.

THE TREATMENT OF PROBLEM DRINKERS - SOME NEW DIRECTIONS

In essence therefore the treatment of problem drinkers is in a state of transition. The early enthusiasm for group based intensive psychotherapeutic regimens has, in the light of consistently negative evaluations, waned. There is a growing awareness that treatment as a commodity cannot be demonstrated as a powerful force in the remission process and that the characteristics the individual client brings to treatment are important in that comparatively minimal intervention can be effective if the client's social milieu is intact. In the short term, the attractiveness of the community based worker in being the deliverer of minimal forms of intervention is very high. The very location of the primary workers' endeavours enhances the possibility of early detection and the exploitation of the advantages that accrue from working with relatively intact clients. Furthermore, the fact that many primary care workers (especially the general practitioner, the health visitor and in some cases the social worker) have an established and on-going relationship with their caseloads may be of importance in minimising treatment drop-out.

However, as noted in the opening paragraph of this paper, many primary care workers are reluctant to become involved in any intervention with problem drinkers. In this regard the work of Shaw, Cartwright, Spratley and Harwin[19] is of importance because they have demonstrated that this reluctance stems from the concern of such workers about their ability to cope with problem drinkers, the legitimacy of their role and the availability of adequate support from colleagues should difficulties arise.

SOME NEW DIRECTIONS (1) - THE MOVE IN TO THE COMMUNITY

Shaw et al[19] have proposed that a network of Community Alcohol Teams (known as CATs) be established and that the prime function of these agencies should be the education and support of front-line workers. It was originally envisaged that such CATs made up of specialist alcohol problem personnel would advise primary care workers on the management of their cases. It was hoped that by offering very good support and supervision the community worker would be encouraged to intervene with problem drinking clients and thus gradually gain experience and confidence.

In the event the establishment of CATs has been a haphazard and somewhat chaotic event with a divergence of opinion existing about just how such agencies should operate. In general, two types of CAT appear to exist. The first which is close to the original specifications of Shaw et al[19] restricts its operation to education of primary care workers about alcohol problems in general and offers to support such workers in terms of giving advice and supervision should difficulties in the management of clients arise. The second type of CAT, which is more common, offers this service but also takes direct referrals from front-line workers. As may be realised this direct work with clients is something of a contradiction of the original aims of CATs in that the emphasis was upon shifting intervention away from specialists and minimising the belief that specialist intervention was the optimum procedure. However, in some cases, it has been found that in order to initiate contact with the very front-line workers the CATs wish to serve it has been necessary to gain credibility by offering a direct referral service and then devolve the treatment of problem drinkers onto the community based workers.

At present there are approximately twenty CATs in operation in Britain but the very recent advent of such services means that the effectiveness of this concept is unknown. However, various evaluations are being undertaken of which the most extensive is that being conducted by Clement in Manchester[20].

SOME NEW DIRECTIONS (2) - SELF HELP MANUALS

This move into the community and the emphasis on the early detection of problem drinkers is also reflected in two recent initiatives being piloted in Scotland. The first of these projects is a combination of Miller's self-management manual approach and the move to engage primary care workers in the provision of services. Designed specifically for general practitioners, this initiative (known as the Drams project - Drinking Reasonably and Moderately) involves the education of family doctors in the use of a short self-help manual. The idea is that if a general practitioner suspects that a patient is drinking excessively then she/he can broach the subject by asking the patient to read the self-help manual and for a fortnight keep a record of alcohol intake. In addition, a blood test may be taken to determine the extent, if any, of liver damage and the results of the drinking diary and blood test are then discussed with the patient. The manual contains information about the alcoholic strength of various beverages, a space for the patient to prepare drinking rules (i.e. the when, where and how much to drink) and helpful suggestions about monitoring alcohol consumption and reducing intake to safe levels.

Given the well recorded reluctance of general practitioners to become involved in any type of alcohol counselling[21], this project has been designed to fit in with general practitioners' demand for a brief, readily applied procedure which is consistent with their normal prescription based method of patient contact. The project is being evaluated[22] and should the initially favourable results be maintained then the development of similar manuals tailored to the needs of other primary care workers is very likely.

The second Scottish project with its emphasis upon early intervention is an innovative and imaginative scheme which reflects the very considerable changes in the delivery of treatment for problem drinkers that has occurred over the past two decades. This study, which is being conducted by Heather, Whitton and Robertson[23], quite simply involved the placing of an advertisement in several Scottish newspapers in early 1983. The advertisement comprised a heading - Are You Drinking Too Much? - and advice about from where free alcohol information was available. Although the advertisement only appeared for a short period (about four insertions in a national daily paper) it attracted over 750 replies. The interest of this investigation lies in the fact that the advertisement also contained the information that the literature available was not for 'alcoholics' but for people who were becoming concerned about their alcohol intake.

One half of the respondents received a straightforward booklet about alcohol and alcohol problems whilst the remainder received a well produced self-help manual, which contained advice about safe drinking and self control strategies for reducing alcohol consumption.

All respondents were also sent a short questionnaire concerning their current alcohol intake, extent of problems associated with their drinking and a general life problems inventory. Perhaps not surprisingly the return rate of the questionnaires was not as high as the investigators may have wished (being 31%) but the return of these questionnaires was sufficient to allow a follow-up study to be conducted. The results of this initial follow-up are without doubt encouraging. Irrespective of whether respondents received the self-help manual or more general alcohol literature, alcohol consumption fell by two-thirds and 60% of those drinking at pre-determined 'unsafe' levels were found on follow-up to be within weekly consumption levels designated as safe. Furthermore, the group receiving the self-help manual reported a larger overall drop in alcohol consumption and a significant reduction (as compared to the control group) on a number of the items in the life problems inventory. The manual was also reported by respondents to be easy to read, useful and was generally better rated than the more general control literature. An additional follow-up study involving interview and collaborative techniques is to be conducted and it will be of interest to see whether the initial positive results are repeated. Obviously if such improvements are maintained then the extension of this type of approach is justified.

In terms of cost effectiveness this intervention with no direct therapist/client contact, is of obvious value and it is not difficult to envisage various applications of this self-help manual approach. For example, this scheme could be applied via the local Councils on Alcoholism network or by Health Authorities through their Health Education departments. The shift of focus in this study, from a treatment to an education based philosophy reflects a fundamental change in the provision of services for problem drinkers and further emphasises the movement away from psychiatrically dominated services and concepts of problem drinkers as being persons in need of intensive and highly specialised care.

However, having noted that the Heather et al study[23] is significant because it does reflect current changes within the alcohol problems intervention field, it would be mistaken to believe that all new initiatives are community based. No matter how good community focussed interventions become, there will always exist a pool of more deteriorated and disadvantaged problem drinkers who will for one reason or another move beyond being readily susceptible to straightforward, minimal advice and education.

In order to highlight developments in practice in this area it is perhaps relevant to cite work concerned with two aspects of counselling problem drinkers which have traditionally been viewed as being especially difficult or troublesome areas for counsellors. Again such work reflects subtle shifts in treatment philosophy as well as being of considerable practical importance.

SOME NEW APPROACHES TO OLD PROBLEMS (1) - MOTIVATION

The first area to consider is the question of motivation. It has often been noted, usually by somewhat disenchanted counsellors that 'alcoholics' lack motivation. As Davies[24] in a short and elegant paper has noted, what this usually means is that the client has behaved in a way different to that advised by his/her therapist. Davies argues that rather than being indicative of 'no motivation' this contrary behaviour just represents motivation to behave in a different manner. Many people come into treatment contact with conflicting attitudes about their problem behaviour; whilst recognising that drinking is associated with long term problems, they also acknowledge that in the short term alcohol provides many benefits, even if only to minimise uncomfortable feelings or fears. This ambivalence is typical of addiction behaviour in general, since it is the individual's selection of short term rewards over possible long term adverse consequences which is the hallmark of such behaviour. Is it therefore a legitimate source of therapist irritation or surprise if people who come for help about an addictive condition actually exhibit the 'symptoms' of their state by electing to indulge in some short term relief? As Davies[24] explains motivation is not stuff which the therapist pours into a client, but is more usefully conceived of as a term used to describe the various factors that influence an individual's decision to select either abstention or to continue to use alcohol excessively.

Miller[25] has taken this debate further by noting that motivation can be viewed as a balance or a seesaw and that the therapist's responsibility is to enhance or facilitate those influences which will tip the balance towards the making, by the client, of a positive resolution to abstain or to reduce alcohol intake to a safe level. The importance of this type of debate is that motivation is not construed as a static entity which clients either have or have not, but is rather a product of counselling and the client's interaction with his or her social milieu. Thus the therapist is responsible for creating a climate in which 'positive motivation' may accrue. It is not therefore totally the client's responsibility to be 'motivated' to alter their drinking behaviour nor totally the client's fault should he or she continue to drink in a damaging manner. Within this framework of joint therapist/client responsibility for motivation the traditional psychotherapeutic cry that the patient is not motivated is no longer available - but the requirement to orchestrate or enhance motivation is.

In Miller's recent work on motivational interviewing[25] a number of useful strategies are proposed which, whilst still requiring formal evaluation, do appear to have considerable clinical utility. Not the least significant of Miller's proposals is that 'denial' of problems is more a reflection of the way in which therapists engage with their clients rather than any pre-existing peculiar characteristic of addicted persons. Miller notes that there is considerable social psychology literature available which indicates that the least effective means of influencing an individual's decision making is to conduct an adversarial debate. In such an interaction one participant (the therapist) presents an array of facts which are critical of or detrimental to the self-esteem or self concept of the other actor (the client). In such a situation the 'defamed' individual inevitably reacts to the presentation of this amalgam of criticism defensively, fending off any criticisms which are not totally accurate and presenting in a better light those accusations that are in the main true. Thus the client is forced into a position of arguing a case in which the putative facts are re-interpreted in a personally more favourable and more comfortable manner. For the therapist to then challenge this interpretation of events with the intent of breaking down the client's 'denial' and giving the client 'insight' into their condition is seldom successful. The therapist is perceived as being anti-client, whilst the client is left arguing a case in which he or she is not as black as is being painted. As Miller has succinctly noted it is a psychological law that 'one believes what one hears oneself speak'. Thus rather than giving the client insight the usual outcome of an adversarial interviewing stance is that the client departs from the interview believing that he or she really is not as bad as everyone else is trying to make out. Miller has suggested that the emphasis in interviewing should be upon facilitating the client's enunciation of concern about his/her drinking and by so doing encourage a dialogue in which the client, not the counsellor, argues the case for the existence of an alcohol problem. This is a very different therapeutic stance from that normally taken in addiction counselling and one that is alien to many established counsellors. However clinical trials involving this type of procedure are being undertaken with some early indications of success[26]. This process of re-appraisal of well accepted counselling precepts is also evident in recent work about another problem area in addiction counselling - that of relapse.

SOME NEW APPROACHES TO OLD PROBLEMS (2) - RELAPSE

Although it is well known that addiction problems, be they to do with smoking, dieting or giving up excessive drinking, are relapsing conditions, little has been done to help patients prevent or minimise their relapses. In fact a number of commentators have noted (e.g. see[27][28]) that relapse as an issue is almost totally ignored, largely because it is felt that any consideration or discussion of relapse with clients is tantamount to tempting providence. Yet all the evidence is that over a one year period in any group of persons resolved to abstain from any problematic behaviour, some 90-95% will to some extent at least break their vow of abstention. It is relevant to emphasise that such vow breaking exists in degrees and it has been accurately noted that any re-use of alcohol by an abstainer can be viewed as a lapse, a relapse or a collapse. Thus it is necessary to be careful about the definition of relapse and considering relapse as a temporary failure in an individual's resolution to abstain (or curtail consumption) has the advantage of allowing a broad perspective to be taken.

Part of this reluctance to address the problem of relapsing clients stems from the past acceptance of the disease model of alcoholism. Within this framework it was generally conceived that once the first drink was consumed then an irresistable biological compulsion to drink until drunk was initiated. If the first drink was 'explained' as being due to craving, then the phenomenon of relapse was understood. Given this type of thinking it is not surprising that relapse was considered a subject best avoided, since the mechanisms that supposedly caused relapse were beyond individual control. However, as the limitations of the disease model became evident two workers, Litman[27] and Marlatt[28] independently produced models of relapse which have considerable relevance for clinical practice.

Although differing in emphasis both Litman and Marlatt have stressed that relapse occurs because of an interaction between individual and situational factors. Marlatt's model is essentially two-staged - with the first stage being concerned with the first drink after a period of abstinence and the second stage the second and further drinks. In the first stage, an individual's resolution to abstain may falter because he or she encounters a situation which exceeds their current levels of coping skill. This inability to cope is perceived by the individual abstainer, and the attractiveness of having a drink (in order to cope in the short term) is naturally increased. Should drinking occur then the individual is confronted with the further difficulty of having broken an important vow and may well attribute this failure of resolution to a lack of self-control (I'm weak-willed) or to a failure of treatment (I'm not cured yet). Whichever the attribution, such thinking with its inherent passive acceptance of the situation is likely to prompt further drinking. Although Marlatt's model has been criticised[29] the importance of this model is that because the explanation of relapse is essentially to do with cognitive and behavioural factors (which are open to influence) rather than biological (and thus more immutable) factors, a range of possible relapse prevention and management techniques becomes available. For example, Annis[30] has recently produced a dangerous situations assessment questionnaire which can be used to increase clients' awareness of the situations in which they personally are most at risk of taking a drink. Also, Allsop, Saunders and McNamee[26] are currently testing out the value of problem solving skills techniques as a means of evolving strategies which may assist clients in coping with dangerous situations.

However, perhaps the most innovative work currently being undertaken is that of Rankin, Hodgson and Stockwell[31]. Working from a social learning theory of dependence, Rankin et al[31] have suggested that parallels can be made between the behavioural treatment of obsessional clients and alcohol problems. A vital element in the successful treatment of obsessional conditions is cue exposure and response prevention. Basically, this is a technique in which after the exposure of the patient to a situation which normally triggers off an obsessional ritual (e.g. contamination by dirt) the response which the patient normally makes (e.g. elaborate hand washing) is prevented. Patients are encouraged to resist the urge to wash and are aided in this resistance by the use of distraction techniques, relaxation and encouragement from their counsellor. Rankin et al[31] have recently applied this technique to alcohol problems. In this procedure, patients were first primed with two drinks of their favourite alcoholic beverage, sufficient in dose to establish a peak blood alcohol level at between 65-100mg/%. Patients were then offered a third drink but were requested to resist the urge to consume. Temptation was increased by having patients at first view the available alcohol, then hold the glass containing alcohol and finally sniff the drink whilst holding it near to the mouth. Patients experienced considerable difficulty in refraining from use, but over the exposure sessions their difficulty in resisting a desire for alcohol decreased and their reduction was significantly greater than patients in a control group.

Experiments such as these which are aimed at improving patients' ability to resist after ingestion of alcohol are of considerable importance not just because of their relevance in tackling a core issue, that of loss of control, but also because they represent the fundamental change that has occurred within alcohol studies. These types of studies which are methodologically sound, theoretically important and clinically relevant would not have been possible two decades ago, when the self-perpetuating and static disease model of alcoholism was predominant and the nature of alcohol problems was considered as being explained. Furthermore, the actual use of alcohol in the treatment of 'alcoholics' was considered unethical. Yet if patients are to learn self mastery over alcohol then there is surely a place in the overall treatment response for patients to learn to cope with the actual substance that causes them so many problems?

SOME CONCLUDING COMMENT

Over the past two decades there has been a radical revision of the way in which alcohol problems are perceived and there has been a major re-appraisal as to how such problems may best be counselled. The result is that many primary care workers, who in the past were at best casual observers of the alcohol problems field, now find themselves being urged to take on a more central role. The test of the next decade is whether the existing alcohol specialists can convince their community based peers that this devolution of counselling problem drinkers is necessary, desirable and feasible.

This move into the community will only occur if primary care workers appreciate the relevance of such a development and have sufficient confidence in their own abilities to take up the challenge. The initial signs are encouraging. The development of more straightforward and practical intervention techniques, with an increasing emphasis on educational rather than mystical psychotherapeutic procedures, augurs well for this transition of responsibility, especially as recent evidence shows that such procedures are effective and have considerable utility. In addition the growing network of Community Alcohol Teams means that any initial shortfall in confidence or knowledge may be overcome and with this an appreciation established that counselling problem drinkers is the business of the primary care worker.

Acknowledgement

This paper has benefited from the comments and endeavours of Stephen Allsop and Georgina Barr.

References

1. Cartwright, A., Shaw, S. & Spratley, T. *Designing a Comprehensive Community Response to Problems of Alcohol Abuse*. Report to the Department of Health and Social Security by the Maudsley Alcohol Pilot Project. The Maudsley Hospital, London, 1975.

2. The Advisory Committee on Alcoholism. *The Pattern and Range of Services for Problem Drinkers*. H.M.S.O., London, 1979.

3. The Scottish Council on Alcoholism. *The Development of Services*. Scottish Council on Alcoholism, Edinburgh, 1975.

4. World Health Organisation Expert Committee on Mental Health. *Technical Report.* Series No. 42, World Health Organisation, Geneva, 1951.

5. Room, R. 'The Measurement and Distribution of Drinking Patterns and Problems in General Populations' in Edwards, G., Gross, M., Keller, M., Moser, J. & Room, R. (Eds.) *Alcohol Related Disabilities.* World Health Organisation, Geneva, 1977.

6. Costello, R. 'Alcoholism Treatment and Evaluation. In Search of Methods II, Collation of Two-Year Follow-up Studies' *International Journal of Addictions.* 10, 1975, 857-865.

7. Costello, R. 'Alcoholism Treatment Effectiveness: Slicing the Outcome Variance Pie' in Edwards, G. & Grant, M., *Alcoholism Treatment in Transition.* Croom Helm, London, 1980.

8. Doroff, D. 'Group Psychotherapy in Alcoholism' in Kissin, B. & Begleiter, M. (Eds.) *The Biology of Alcoholism.* Volume 5, Plenum Press, New York, 1977.

9. Armor, D., Polich, J. & Stambul, H. *Alcoholism and Treatment.* Wiley, New York, 1978.

10. Levinson, T. & Sereny, G. 'An Experimental Evaluation of Insight Therapy for the Chronic Alcoholic' *Canadian Psychiatric Association Journal.* 14, 1969, 143-146.

11. Ritson, B. & Hassal, C. *The Management of Alcoholism.* Livingston Press, Edinburgh, 1970.

12. Orford, J. & Edwards, G. *Alcoholism.* Oxford University Press, London, 1971.

13. Emrick, C. 'A Review of Psychologically Oriented Treatment of Alcoholsim II. The relative effectiveness of different treatment approaches and the effectiveness of treatment versus no treatment' *Journal of Studies on Alcohol.* 36, 1975, 88-108.

14. Clare, A. 'How Good is Treatment?' in Edwards, G. & Grant, M. *Alcoholism.* Croom Helm, London, 1977.

15. Miller, W. & Hester, R. 'Treating the Problem Drinker; Modern Approaches' in Miller, W. (Ed.) *The Addictive Behaviours.* Pergamon Press, 1980.

16. Miller, W. & Taylor, C. 'Relative Effectiveness of Bibliotherapy, Individual and Group Self-Control Training in the Treatment of Problem Drinkers' *Addictive Behaviours.* 5, 1980, 13-24.

17. Miller, W., Taylor, C. & West, J. 'Focussed Versus Broad Spectrum Behaviour Therapy for Problem Drinkers' *Journal of Consulting and Clinical Psychology.* 48, 1980, 590-601.

18. Plant, M. & Plant, M. 'Self Reported Alcohol Consumption and other Characteristics of 100 Patients Attending a Scottish Alcoholism Treatment Unit' *British Journal on Alcohol and Alcoholism.* 14, 1979, 197-207.

19. Shaw, S., Cartwright, A., Spratley, T. & Harwin, J. *Responding to Drinking Problems.* Croom Helm, London, 1979.

20. Clement, S. The Salford Community Alcohol Team - an Evaluation. Paper presented at the 18th Scottish Alcohol Research Symposium, Pitlochry, Scotland, April, 1984.

21. Wilkins, R. *The Hidden Alcoholic in General Practice.* Elek Science, London, 1974.

22. Glen, I. The DRAMS Project. Paper presented at the 16th Scottish Alcohol Research Symposium, Pitlochry, Scotland, April, 1983.

23. Heather, N., Witton, B. & Robertson, I. 'Evaluation of a Self-Help Manual for Media Recruited Problem Drinkers: 6 month follow-up results'. Unpublished paper, Department of Psychiatry, University of Dundee, 1984.

24. Davies, J. 'A Psychological Look at Willpower and Motivation' *Salud* 1. 1982, 13-19.

25. Miller, W. 'Motivational Interviewing with Problem Drinkers' *Behavioural Psychotherapy.* 11, 1983, 147-172.

26. Allsop, S., Saunders, W. & McNamee, B. Relapse Prevention and Management. Report to the Alcohol Education and Research Council - 1st Year Report of a Clinical Trial. Alcohol Studies Centre, 1984.

27. Litman, G. 'Relapse in Alcoholism: Traditional and Current Approaches' in Edwards, G. & Grant, M. (Eds.) *Alcoholism Treatment in Transition.* Croom Helm, London, 1980.

28. Marlatt, G. 'Craving for Alcohol, Loss of Control and Relapse' in Nathan, P.E., Marlatt, G. & Loberg, T. (Eds.) *Alcoholism - New Directions in Behavioural Research and Treatment.* Plenum Press, London, 1978.

29. Saunders, W. & Allsop, S. 'From Theory to Practice: A Consideration of the Marlatt Relapse Model' in Curson, D. & Rankin, H. (Eds.) *Alcoholism Relapse.* Logos, Alpha, London, 1984.

30. Annis, H. 'A Relapse Prevention Model for Treatment of Alcoholics' in Curson, D. & Rankin, H. (Eds.) *Alcoholism Relapse.* Logos, Alpha, London, 1984.

31. Rankin, H., Hodgson, R. & Stockwell, T. 'Cue Exposure and Response Prevention with Alcoholics: A Controlled Trial' *Behavioural Research Therapy.* 21, 4, 1983, 435-446.

Alcohol Problems and the Family

Jim Orford

When considering the involvement of families in alcohol problems it is important to appreciate that this topic can be considered from a variety of very divergent perspectives. Families complicated by excessive drinking have, for example, been viewed as examples of *families in crisis* experiencing the same sorts of symptoms of insecurity, social isolation, and change of roles within the family as do families facing other kinds of crisis such as unemployment, wartime separation, and mental illness[1]. Alternatively such families can be viewed from a *cultural patterning perspective* concerned with the historical and cultural roots of family life which have determined, amongst other things, the sexual and economic restraints upon family members in a particular social group or sub group[2]. A further alternative is an *ecological* view which emphasises the family's present economic and social context including such important concerns as employment, finances, housing, and child-care[3]. Yet another viewpoint is that of *contagion* theory which is concerned with the effects upon the family of such things as rising national consumption of alcohol, the contagious spread of new patterns of drinking behaviour, and the availability to family members of outlets for the purchase of alcohol[4]. These views are not incompatible, but it is difficult to think and operate within more than one or two of them at a time, and it is important to know which model of alcohol and the family one is working with.

The two most influential models for those involved in treatment are the *stress victim* and the *systems* perspectives, and the first two sections of this chapter will examine research that has been carried out within these two seemingly contradictory frameworks. The third section will then consider research on treatment involving family members and the chapter will conclude by making tentative recommendations about approaches to and treatment of families with alcohol problems.

FAMILY MEMBERS AS VICTIMS OF STRESS

This view supposes that the drinking problem of one member has a stressful impact upon other members of the family who then search for ways of responding or coping, which in turn may be relatively functional or dysfunctional as the case may be. The non-excessively drinking members of the family are important, according to this model, because they themselves are at risk because of the stress they are under, and because the ways in which they react may have a bearing upon the future course of the drinking problem.

Marital Unhappiness and Separation

A number of investigators have assessed the degree of 'hardship' to which a spouse (almost always a wife married to an excessively drinking husband in these studies) has been exposed as a result of the partner's excessive drinking. Studies in Britain[5], the USA[6][7], and in a number of other countries including Finland[8] and Japan[9], have found that women married to men with identified drinking problems very often describe a great deal of severe, and often longstanding, hardship. This includes concern over the husband's job and economic security, financial strain, social embarrassment, reduction of social contacts, failure to keep up personal appearances, rows and quarrels, a poor sex life and infidelity, possessiveness and jealousy directed towards the wife, damage to household objects or furniture, physical violence in the family, and involvement with police.

It is equally clear from these studies, however, that this hardship is a variable quantity. It is important not to make sweeping generalisations about 'alcoholic marriages', just as it is important not to make unsupported generalisations about all 'alcoholics' or problem drinkers. In one study of 100 London couples, where the husbands were under treatment for drinking problems[5], we discovered wide variation in the degree of marital cohesion. Some couples reported low levels of mutual affection (on the Marital Patterns Test[10]), and wives expressed a generally negative view of their husbands using expressions such as:

'. . . hate him . . . unable to forgive him . . . never loved him . . . my feelings are dead . . . feeling of deep revulsion . . . drinking is not the main problem . . . it's his person I don't like . . .'. These attitudes were often associated with pessimism about, and lack of understanding of, the husband's behaviour, combined with resignation about the future. These cases, however, were extreme ones along a dimension at the other end of which were those couples who reported high levels of affection and where wives made a clear distinction between their husbands' unacceptable behaviour when drinking and their appropriate behaviour when not drinking. As we shall see later, in the section on Partners' Involvement in Treatment, these differences in marital cohesion are related to treatment outcome.

One research strategy used in studies in Britain[5] and the USA[11][12] has been to consider marital roles. Complaints on grounds of role failure are made over things large and small. Many problem drinking husbands were found in these studies to be less involved in housework, or in doing repairs around the home, than either they or their wives considered ideal. Many were accused of not 'being around' when needed by the family. Although there was a general under-involvement in family 'tasks', however, there was no such under-involvement (indeed in some cases a suggestion of over- influence) in family 'decisions' about social recreational life and about marital sexual behaviour. Again the existence of great variation between couples needs to be stressed. It is also important to bear in mind that the kinds of stresses and marital unhappiness described by those who have studied families with alcohol problems are not unique and occur in other families also. The dangers of viewing the study of alcohol problems and the family as a specialism divorced from the study of marital problems generally have been pointed out before[13].

The possible connection between excessive drinking and family violence is a matter that has attracted special research attention. In our study of 100 couples[5], 72 per cent of wives reported sometimes being threatened by their husbands, 45 per cent having ever been beaten by them, and 27 per cent ever having experienced their husband attempting to injure them seriously. Others have adopted the strategy of asking battered women about their husbands' drinking. In one British study[14], 100 battered women reported a high rate (50 per cent regularly drunk) of problem drinking amongst their husbands. In a similar study in the USA[15] which focussed on battering incidents themselves, 16 per cent of battered women reported excessive drinking by their husbands during all of the four battering incidents which they were asked to describe. On the other hand only 19 per cent were thought not to have been drinking during any of the four incidents, the majority showing an inconsistent pattern of alcohol use or excess across the four occasions. Another study of those (mostly women) appearing in a Canadian Family Court found reports of violence to be more than twice as likely when an alcohol problem was said to exist in the family[16].

Research suggests that we are right to suppose that wives living with men with drinking problems are at risk of experiencing distress and disturbance themselves. In addition to the kinds of hardship already described, there is the uncertainty that many family members describe about knowing whether there really is a problem in the family or not, deciding whether it is a problem of their own making or of someone else's, deciding what exactly the problem is, and in then deciding how is the best way to respond. These uncertainties were described in the classic research report by Jackson[17] thirty years ago. 'Alcoholism' or 'problem drinking' may now be more available to family members as ways of construing what is going wrong, but it is unlikely that this has reduced feelings of uncertainty very greatly. In one study[18] wives of problem drinkers were asked a series of questions about psychosomatic symptoms which had previously been used in the large-scale Midtown Manhattan Survey of mental health in New York. Sixty-five per cent of wives who were at the time of the study living with a husband who was drinking excessively, were at least moderately disturbed according to this scale, and 43 per cent living with a husband whose drinking had once been excessive but which was no longer so, were also at least moderately disturbed. These figures compared with 35 per cent in the Midtown Survey. Those whose husbands had stopped drinking, or who had become separated in the meantime, reported less disturbance the longer the time that had elapsed.

Rates of marital breakdown are high when a serious drinking problem exists for one or other partner, indeed many observers of families with alcohol problems have expressed surprise that so many such marriages survive at all. Survival of marriages is less surprising, however, if one considers the many obvious barriers against marital breakdown such as felt obligations to children, moral restraints, external pressure from relatives or the local community, legal difficulties, and a wife's lack of independent source of income, and an absence of anyone to take the partner's place[19]. Research has suggested that spouses are more likely to seek outside help, and are more likely to take action which leads to the termination of their marriage, if the level of hardship or deviance experienced is relatively high[7][12][20]. Just to stress again the probable non-uniqueness of marriages with alcohol problems, it should be noted that one of these studies[12] found that it was the most general aspects of hardship in marriage, namely 'non-performance of socio-emotional roles' (husband not a good companion; husband not a good father; husband not a comfort and support to wife) which were most closely associated with seeking separation or divorce.

Although at least one in three of those seeking help for drinking problems are now women, there has been a regrettable lack of research on husbands married to women problem drinkers. One review[21] came to only one tentative conclusion, namely that there is a high prevalence of excessive drinking amongst such husbands themselves. A Swedish study comparing married men and married women with drinking problems, treated in the 1960s and followed up for between six and twelve years, provides some interesting information however[22]. This study also found a high percentage (50 per cent) of husbands of women problem drinkers having drinking problems themselves. Sixty per cent of the marriages of women problem drinkers were described as 'serious conflicts, divorce discussed', in comparison with 35 per cent of the marriages of male problem drinkers. Thirty-nine per cent of partners in the former group were described as 'understanding' versus 65 per cent in the latter, and the percentages of partners who were 'strongly disapproving' were 55 per cent and 27 per cent respectively. Although the marriages of the women problem drinkers emerged as less satisfactory, and husbands as less sympathetic than wives of male problem drinkers, at follow-up the percentages of marriages surviving intact (32 per cent and 35 per cent respectively) were similar. More of the marriages of women problem drinkers had been terminated by death of one partner or the other, and somewhat more of the marriages of men problem drinkers by divorce or separation.

Children as Victims

Until quite recently the possible stresses experienced by children living in families with alcohol problems had been relatively neglected. Indeed Margaret Cork entitled the report of the early interview study of 115 youngsters *The Forgotten Children*[23]. Recently a great deal more interest has been shown and research has at least begun to outline the links of stresses to which such children are particularly prone. One of the most obvious of these is chronic exposure to a poor family atmosphere, with much parental marital tension and discord, and disruption of joint family activities and rituals[23][24][25]. In fact 98 of Cork's 115 children reported 'parental fighting and quarrelling' as their main concern in comparison with only seven who gave 'drinking' or 'drunkenness' as their main worry. Once again, the fact that the stresses in families with alcohol problems are in the main not specific to such families is made abundantly clear.

On the other hand, there may be forms of stress which are unusually common amongst children of families with drinking problems. One candidate which has been suggested as a result of interviews with such young people (eg [23][26]) is a restriction on meeting friends or reciprocating invitations because of embarrassment about parental behaviour. It appears that this is something that such children often describe, but whether it is specific to such families and whether it leads to a distortion of friendship formation, as has been suggested, is not proven.

Again it is important to remind ourselves that 'children of alcoholics' are far from being a homogenous group: circumstances vary greatly and generalisations should be treated with great caution. For one thing, length of exposure to a parental drinking problem during childhood, and the age at which exposure takes place, are obviously variables of significance. Furthermore, excessive drinking patterns vary greatly. Some children are regularly exposed to parental drunkenness, whilst others are shielded from it although their parent may have a very serious problem[26]. Another variable is the amount of violence experienced. As a group, children in families with drinking problems undoubtedly witness and personally experience more family violence than the average, but not all do so. One study found that it was those boys and girls whose problem drinking father was also violent who were particularly at risk of developmental disorder[27].

Preliminary data from an interview study of young adults in their late teens, twenties, or early thirties who had had a parent with a drinking problem are shown in Table 1. These show much higher rates of recalled family violence for the family alcohol problems group than for the comparison group, and particularly so for parent-parent violence, but they also show that only a minority recall violence that was serious or more than occasional[28].

A whole range of ill-effects has been reported for children of excessively drinking parents. For example, compared to control groups, they have been found to show a high incidence of school problems, difficulty in concentrating, conduct problems and truancy from school, poor school performance, and need for special or remedial schools. They have also been reported to show elevated rates of emotional problems, such as anxiety and depression, and of developmental disorders, as well as fewer means of coping with emotional upset. Other reports have shown them to become intoxicated more often than controls, and themselves to have drinking and drug problems. On the other hand, others have been impressed at how small are the differences between groups; one report has found no difference between children of excessive drinkers and controls in terms of 'personality disturbance' as measured by anxiety, depression and social isolation, and another reported no difference in the rate of attendance at psychiatric clinics. These findings have been reviewed on a number of occasions[24][29]. Harmful effects appear to be more regularly reported for young children than for adolescents.

Quite apart from ill-effects upon young children and adolescents, there is evidence, largely from retrospective self-report studies with clinical groups, that children of excessively drinking parents are themselves more than usually at risk of developing drinking problems in adulthood. This work has been thoroughly reviewed by Goodwin[30] and Cotton[31] who concluded that alcohol problems do indeed run in families. Present evidence therefore suggests that children of problem drinkers represent an important high risk group both because of their proneness to problems during childhood and adolescence, and their proneness to problems in later life.

TABLE 1

*Percentage of 16-35 year old children of problem drinking
parents, and comparisons, who recall family violence
during their upbringing*

	Children of Problem Drinkers % (N = 168)	Comparisons % (N = 81)
Parent to parent violence		
Serious and regular violence, over a prolonged period	12	1
Any serious and regular violence	12.5	1
Any serious and prolonged violence	21	1
Any regular and prolonged violence	26	4
Any serious violence	29	7
Any regular violence	27	5
Any prolonged violence	48	6
Any violence	66	21
Parent to self violence		
Serious and regular violence, over a prolonged period	9	4
Any serious and regular violence	11	5
Any serious and prolonged violence	14	6
Any regular and prolonged violence	18	5
Any serious violence	20	10
Any regular violence	21	6
Any prolonged violence	30	15
Any violence (excluding controlled corporal punishment)	41	19
Any violence (including controlled corporal punishment)	59	77

Genetic transmission may provide part of the explanation for any inter-generation transmission of drinking problems which exists. It is difficult to draw certain conclusions from research to date, but recent reviews[32][33] report that twin and adoption studies, although not entirely consistent in their findings, have produced some evidence for a genetic component at least in the determination of male drinking behaviour.

Again variability needs to be stressed. One important fact about children of problem drinking parents is that many, perhaps the majority, appear to escape obviously harmful ill-effects[32].

Other Family Members as Victims

Although most of the research has been conducted on wives and children as victims, with rather less on husbands, practitioners will regularly meet family members who are affected by the excessive drinking of a relative but who have not been the subject of research. These will include parents of teenagers and young adults who drink excessively, and the middle-aged children and children-in- law of elderly parents who are now recognised to be at least as liable to excessive drinking as other age groups[34]. Practitioners also find that when a serious drinking problem exists in the family, relatives other than partners and children often become embroiled in the problem and their influence may be for good or ill[35].

Finally, in this section on family members as victims of excessive drinking, we should include the unborn foetus. There is now a substantial and growing body of research which appears to show, not only that regular excessive drinking during pregnancy can lead to a syndrome of growth retardation, central nervous system damage, and characteristic facial features, in the newborn infant (the Foetal Alcohol Syndrome), but also that any drinking other than extremely light drinking during pregnancy may lead to low birth weight and other signs of FAS in mild degree[36][37]. The exact picture is complicated by the effects of nutrition during pregnancy, use of nicotine and other drugs, and the possibility that heavy alcohol consumption by the father may cause genetic damage.

A FAMILY SYSTEMS PERSPECTIVE

The stress victim model assigns clear roles to different family members: one is the excessive drinker, the rest receive the impact and are at risk of suffering ill-effects as a result. There are a number of research findings which are troublesome to such a viewpoint however. One of these, already mentioned, is that drinking is often heavy or excessive in a second member of the family, particularly when the wife is the identified 'problem drinker'. Another, emerging from the studies of marital roles[5][11], is that role performance is sometimes reported to be non-ideal even in the early months of marriage, and that many partners married in the knowledge of heavy or excessive drinking. Another indication of the complexity of the matter was the demonstration that wives' levels of stress and current symptoms were not independent of their reports of abnormalities in their own families or upbringing[38].

Clinicians also have long reported that families with alcohol problems are frequently more complicated than the simple stress victim model would suppose. They have, for example, suggested that family members can sometimes be as resistant to treatment progress as the identified excessive drinker. Indeed at one time the leading view of excessive drinking and marriage was that wives married to 'alcoholic' husbands had predictable kinds of disturbed personalities themselves. Such simple misogynist theories have now largely been discredited[21][39].

A systems view of families with alcohol problems is described in a number of reviews[39-43]. It treats the family as an indivisible system of people playing interdependent roles and it eschews the idea of attributing to individuals any particular parts in the drama, such as 'problem person' or 'stress victim'. In systems perspective, the use of alcohol in the family is purposive, adaptive and meaningful. A proper assessment would consider what functions excessive drinking is serving for the family as a whole, not just for the individual identified problem drinker. According to Steinglass[43] whose name is most closely associated with this perspective, these functions include the family's attempts to deal with a problem in some other member of the family, a problem arising between two or more family members, or serious difficulties the family faces in making an adjustment to its immediate social environment. Thus, excessive drinking in one member could well be a signal of a family problem at one or another level. The idea of homeostasis is an important one here for understanding the way in which the family has become stuck in a repetitive pattern involving excessive drinking, and the difficulty the whole family may have in accepting and adjusting to change. Research which has been carried out from this perspective, or which bears strongly upon it, has taken a variety of forms.

Interaction Studies

Steinglass has found support for the systems view as a result of his unique research strategy of simultaneously admitting family members to an experimental residential treatment facility in which periods of drinking and abstinence are alternated and the effects upon family interactions observed. His early work involved a father and son and two pairs of brothers, all chronic excessive drinkers, whilst his later work has involved husbands and wives, at least one of each couple having a drinking problem. Observations revealed dramatic change in patterns of interactional behaviour during intoxication in comparison with those seen during sobriety, but the direction of this change was not always anticipated either by the couples or by the observers. For example:

'... a father and son who had been distant and highly critical of each other while sober expressed warmth, tenderness, and closeness while drinking. A pair of brothers whose past histories seemed liberally sprinkled with episodes of intra-familial violence and psychosocial chaos alternated their drinking patterns so that one brother always remained sober while the other brother drank, and the sober brother exercised the controlling influence on his manifestly drunken sibling' ([43], pp 135-6).

'A couple who predicted an increased tendency toward depression during drinking instead became angry and affectively changed. A couple who described their alcohol symptom as increasing their ability to relate to strangers were noted to become more distant and appear to wall themselves off from other couples once drinking began' (p. 139).

That excessive drinking may serve some positive functions, despite the seemingly harmful effects upon the family, was suggested by some results of our study of 100 couples[5]. Both the husbands (the identified problem drinkers) and their wives were asked to complete an adjective check list to describe the husband's behaviour when drinking, when sober, and 'ideally'. By scoring the check list separately for dominance-submissiveness and affection-hostility, we obtained results for the group of couples as a whole which suggested that drinking might simultaneously have functional effects in terms of dominance and dysfunctional effects in terms of affection. Most of the husbands, and most of their wives, viewed the non-drinking husband as insufficiently affectionate and insufficiently dominant. Both the husbands and wives reported that drinking reduced the level of affection still further below what was considered ideal, but reported that dominance was increased to a near-ideal level.

Other studies have observed couples interacting but in a less naturalistic setting than the simulated home environment of the experimental ward used by Steinglass. In one study[44], for example, couples with a drinking problem were significantly less co-operative and more competitive than control couples when playing a card game deliberately designed to allow for these different ways of interacting. According to one recent review[45], however, at least one unpublished study has failed to replicate this finding. In another study[46] wives of problem drinkers were recorded as looking at their husbands more when discussion focussed upon drinking. However, a later study [47] found that this was the same for couples where the husband had a psychiatric disorder but was not an excessive drinker, but that the two groups did differ in the frequency with which partners interrupted one another in the course of their conversations, problem drinkers and their wives interrupting one another more frequently.

In another interactional study of this kind eight families with a drinking problem (the husband-fathers being the identified problem drinkers in each case) and eight comparison families were recruited through newspaper advertisements. Each family consisted of both parents and at least two children between 10 and 17 years old. The parents were observed interacting alone, and each parent was observed interacting with the two children together. Sessions in which alcohol was available and unavailable were systematically varied[48]. The results are complicated but suggest that problem drinking fathers showed less leadership-assertiveness problem solving behaviour than did control fathers, but that their wives exhibited relatively more of such directive influence than did control mothers. The amount of drinking was not great and there were few differences between drinking and non-drinking conditions, but couples from both groups together communicated more directly with one another when not drinking. This study did not include a group with family problems other than excessive drinking in order to see whether patterns of communication were specific to families with drinking problems. Another study of this kind[49] did include such a group as well as a 'non-distressed couples' control group. A number of differences were found in interactional behaviour (only husbands and wives were involved in this study, again the husbands being the identified problem drinkers), but there were no differences between the couples with drinking problems and the 'non-alcoholic' distressed couples, thus supporting the non-specific hypothesis. The authors of this report summarise their findings by saying:

'Both alcoholic and distressed couples communicated significantly fewer rational problem-solving statements and engaged in more negative and hostile acts than did non-alcoholic, maritally satisfied couples . . . These results suggest that at least some of the problematic marital communications noted in the literature on alcoholics are observed among distressed couples in general and may not reflect problems unique to alcoholics' (p 193).

Although they are not strictly studies of interaction, we should include here research on interperson perception and marriages with drinking problems[50][51]. In the typical study of this kind, partners are asked to describe themselves, their spouses, and sometimes how they think their spouses view them, in terms of some standard personality questionnaire or adjective check list. Certain discrepancy scores are then computed in an attempt to capture aspects of interpersonal sensitivity, understanding or communication. For example, how a husband described his wife could be compared with how the wife described herself and the size of the discrepancy between these two perceptions taken to indicate the degree of lack of sensitivity on the husband's part. In one major Scottish study of this kind[50], a number of significantly larger discrepancies were found amongst couples with drinking problems than amongst a control group of couples. These larger discrepancies involved both spouse perceptions (eg. a comparison of what W thinks of H with what H thinks of himself) as well as 'metaperceptions' (eg. a comparison of what W thinks of H with what H thinks W thinks about him). These results again support the view that many of the experiences of families with alcohol problems are similar to the experiences of distressed and unhappy families generally, because these findings are very like those found in similar studies of couples with problems other than drinking.

INTEGRATING THE SYSTEMS AND STRESS-VICTIM VIEWPOINTS

Although it is important to keep in mind that such apparently different viewpoints are possible, in practice it seems that those with direct experience of families complicated by alcohol problems work with elements of each. Certainly research does not enable us to choose between them, and the two different strands of research have had different strengths and used different samples (much of the early stress-victim research was carried out with the help of Al-Anon wives; much of the systems research with the help of couples seen in a mental health service setting). The danger is probably in adhering too rigidly to one or another extreme viewpoint. Systems thinking alone carries the danger of losing sight of the commonsense approach that partners and children are victims of the excessive drinking with which they must learn to cope in the best possible way, whilst stress-victim thinking alone runs the risk of ignoring the interactional nature of family life and the possible family functions which continued excessive drinking may be serving.

The two models may be reconciled by giving relatively greater weight to one view or the other in different cases. Those who have written from a system perspective[40][52] make it clear that they believe this view is more appropriate in some cases than in others, and as we shall see in the following section those who advocate family therapy based partly upon a system model recommend that it be used selectively[52]. An alternative is to attempt a reconciliation in the form of a single theory. Wilson for example has recently proposed a form of transactional model in which all family members (including the identified problem drinker) are seen as attempting to cope with the stress to which they are exposed, with all such reactions having repercussions for the rest of the family[53]. Such a view acknowledges both the reality of the drinking problem and the interdependence of parts within the whole family system. An important aspect of this is the acceptability of different ways of understanding what is going wrong on the part of family members themselves. A hint of the wide differences that may exist in this respect came from the Swedish follow-up study referred to earlier[22]. Whilst only 20 per cent of married male problem drinkers thought their alcohol problems were partly due to their partners (none thought they were wholly so), no less than 80 per cent of married women problem drinkers felt this way (16 per cent thought their alcohol problem wholly due to their partners).

INVOLVING FAMILIES IN TREATMENT

Naturalistic Coping

Because the large majority of families with drinking problems do not come into direct contact with professional alcohol treatment agencies, it is important to consider the ways in which such families treat themselves. Research asking spouses how they have attempted to cope[54][55] has revealed a number of coping strategies including the following: pleading, threatening, and rowing; avoiding, keeping out of the way; withdrawing sexually; being indulgent (giving a drink to help with the hangover, going without to give the drinker money, etc); controlling access to drink (pouring it away, making a rule not to allow it in the house, etc); attacking or competing; taking greater control or responsibility (eg over money matters or child-care); seeking outside help; and taking steps towards separation.

Similar research with children living in families with alcohol problems[28][53] has shown that they use a very similar range of tactics, although avoidance, and other passive or self-directed responses may be more common than amongst spouses. Data from the first 130 young adults in the study of 16 - 35 year olds referred to earlier[28] are shown in Table 2.

There are no clear prescriptions from research about how to advise those many family members who are in a quandary about how to cope and who wish to find ways of coping better. In our own research on 100 couples, husbands whose wives had been trying to reduce the availability of alcohol by pouring it away

TABLE 2

Recalled childhood coping behaviour of a sample of 16-35 year old children of problem drinking parents

Forms of Coping Behaviour Described	% (N = 130)
Fearful inaction, eg too afraid to do anything; terrified.	21
Fear for the future, eg afraid for the family; worried what would happen in future	23
Switched off, eg built shell around self; day-dreamed; felt lonely	25
Self-blame, eg was a martyr; blamed self; felt guilty	10
Avoidance, eg avoided him/her; refused to talk to him/her; left alone; hid; stayed in bedroom; went out; left home.	55
Indulgence, eg gave him/her a drink; gave him/her money; made him/her comfortable	11
Stoicism, eg pretended all was well; put on a bold front	14
Anti-drink, eg found the drink; poured drink away; hid drink	9
Discord, eg rowed with him/her; pleaded; threatened; hit	39
Emotional attack, eg tried to make him/her jealous; to show him/her up; to make him/her look ridiculous	4
Action against self, eg got drunk; refused to eat; made self sick; threatened to kill self	12
Protective action, eg hid own money; took special care of own possessions	2
Help-seeking, eg sought help from neighbour or relative; escaped next door	18

when they found it or by trying to make rules about drinking at home, did relatively well, and those whose wives had been adopting avoidance or withdrawal strategies did relatively badly[54]. As a result we tentatively recommend 'engaged but discriminating' coping in which family members would remain involved in attempts to help the problem drinker but would direct their attempts at the drink rather than at the drinker. It may well be the case, though, that our results were an artifact, and the different outcomes merely the result of different levels of severity of problem, with wives who avoided their husbands doing so simply because they had more hardships to cope with.

Our conclusions were in any case not totally in line with the kind of advice fairly consistently given in books addressed directly to partners and children[56][57] and by Al-Anon (a self-help organisation, allied to Alcoholics Anonymous, for relatives of excessive drinkers). An analysis of the content of the books by Meyer[56] and Seixas[57] shows that they recommend that spouses and children *be positive* (see the drinking as a symptom, understand the drinker's distress, not moralise, understand it is difficult to stop drinking), that they *do not protect or collude* (eg do not help supply alcohol, or make excuses to others, or otherwise soften the effects of over drinking), and that where possible they should use *constructive confrontation* (eg feed in correct information, leave pamphlets and books around, calmly confront after a crisis, let the excessive drinker know clearly the effects of drinking on you). However, they also recommend a certain detachment. Spouses should *take distance emotionally*, not carry the burden of thinking that they are the cause of the problem, and if necessary consider divorce as the most positive solution[56]. Children should try and 'let go' of their parent's problem, find ways to get away for a while, not feel ashamed, and take responsibility for their own lives[57].

Members of Al-Anon are also taught to 'detach with love' which, according to Harwin[3] means:

'... the individual must try to unravel the tight knot of symbiosis, whereby the spouse's entire life revolves around futile attempts to change the alcoholic. Instead the partner is encouraged to achieve some measure of personal fulfilment so that the need to control the alcohol abuser is reduced and so that some pleasure is introduced into an otherwise unhappy situation' (pp 232-3).

About the only study of how Al-Anon members cope with their problems, in Washington, USA[58], found that the longer the wife had been a member, the less likely she was to use 'negative coping strategies'. These referred not only to such things as coaxing, nagging, pleading, and covering up, but also to such things as pouring drink away, which was found to carry a positive prognosis in our study[54]. Meyer[56] also recommends that spouses do not attempt to control their partners' drinking, and specifically recommends that they not throw drink away ('Do realise he will only buy more' - p 87).

Partners' Involvement in Treatment

There are in fact at least two studies which confirm the clinical impression that treatment for drinking problems proceeds better if a partner can be involved.

One, in North Carolina, USA[59], found that men with drinking problems persisted longer in treatment if their wives were attending a concurrent group, and both this and the other study, from Edinburgh[60], reported greater improvement for men whose wives were involved in concurrent treatment. In the former study, 50 per cent of wives volunteered for the group programme but none of the husbands of women with drinking problems, and others' experience of the difficulty of involving husbands is similar.

It is possible of course that the North Carolina and Edinburgh results were simply due to the better prognosis for those men whose wives were willing to be involved. There is certainly evidence from other research that the prognosis is better when marriages are more cohesive. It was mentioned earlier that marital cohesion varied widely in our study of 100 couples[5]. In the same study husbands from the more cohesive couples did better, being twice as likely as others to have a good outcome a year later. Another study, from the USA[61], found greater conflict and less marital cohesion in the marriages of these problem drinkers with poorer outcome, although in this case it is not clear that the study was done prospectively. In general, however, it can be concluded that there is good evidence that the more cohesive families are, the better the chance of a good outcome. The willingness of other family members to be involved in treatment is probably a reflection of cohesion, but their involvement in the treatment process may strengthen this cohesion and hence improve the chances of a favourable outcome.

Treatment for Families

The problems of carrying out conclusive research on family treatment are formidable. Quite apart from the usual problems of conducting treatment outcome research, there is in addition the difficulty of recruiting sizeable enough samples of cases in which two or more members of a family are willing to become engaged, and remain in treatment. The usual problems of satisfactorily defining 'outcome' are also made more difficult: is it a good outcome if excessive drinking continues but marital communication improves; or if problem drinking ceases but the family breaks up; or if drinking continues but spouse and children become less enmeshed in the problem and their health and happiness improves? These problems are such that reviewers of research on treatment for families with alcohol problems[3][40] can offer us no very clear directions about which forms of family treatment are the most effective.

What these reviews do show, however, is the range of family treatments that have been used. This can be seen in Table 3 which summarises those studies reported by Harwin[3], Steinglass[40], or by both. A number of points emerge.

TABLE 3

Studies of treatment for families with drinking problems

(Based on material reviewed by Harwin[3] and/or Steinglass[40])

(a) *Concurrent Groups*

	Clients	Treatment	Outcome
Gliedman et al[62]	9 wives	45 offered treatment 9 participated in concurrent groups with a style of their own.	No control group; some improvement for most wives
Ewing et al[59]	16 wives	32 wives offered treatment, 16 took part in concurrent groups with the same dynamically oriented psychotherapy style as husbands' groups	Compared with husbands whose wives did not participate, husbands persisted better in treatment and improved more.
Smith[60]	15 wives	23 wives offered treatment, 15 took part in groups while husbands received inpatient treatment	Compared with those husbands whose wives did not participate, husbands showed greater improvement.

(b) *Conjoint Groups*

	Clients	Treatment	Outcome
Burton & Kaplan[63]	227 couples	1-44 sessions focussing on marital conflict not drinking; some received individual counselling first	No control group; of 73% followed up, 56% reduced or stopped excessive drinking, 75% fewer marital problems
Corder et al [64]	20 men + wives	Wives joined husbands for last 4 days of month-long treatment; groups included video analysis of sessions, lectures, role-plays,	Matched control group without wives involved; treatment group significantly better in drinking, employment, and less divorce or

Clients	Treatment	Outcome

(b) Conjoint Groups (Continued)

		recreation, AA and Al-Anon	separation, at 6 months follow-up.
Cadogan [65]	20 both sexes + spouses	Out-patient; 90 minutes once a week; average 5 couples; open groups; focussing on marital problem-solving and communication	Random assignment to immediate treatment or waiting list; at 6 months follow-up 9/20 abstinent (vs 2/20), 4 drinking moderately (vs 5), 7 relapsed (vs 13).
Gallant et al[66]	118 couples	4-7 couples per group; once every 2 weeks for 2 hours; following inpatient treatment for problem drinkers; focussing on inter-actional behaviour	No control group; 24 lost to follow up; 53 'definite successes' at 2-10 months follow up.
Steinglass et al[67]	10 middle class couples (3 wives with drinking problems)	2 weeks 3 sessions per week out-patient; then 10 days inpatient, 3 couples admitted simultaneously, alcohol freely available part of the time; then 3 weeks 2 sessions a week out-patient; then re-convened at 6 week intervals for 6 months; focussing on inter-actional pattern; improved family functioning the primary target; including video, role-play, one-way mirror observations.	8 available at 6 months follow-up; results 'disappointing' (3).

Clients	Treatment	Outcome

(c) *Family Therapy*

	Clients	Treatment	Outcome
Hedburg & Campbell [68]	couples receiving behavioural family counselling (49 couples assigned to BFC and 3 other groups not involving family treatment)	25 sessions; focussing on drinking	Of 26 selecting abstinence as goal, 80% of BFC group achieved abstinence, vs 60% and 36% in 2 other individual behaviour therapy treatment groups
Meeks & Kelly[69]	5 men & wives	During 10-12 months of aftercare following separate treatment for families during 7 week day-treatment programme focus on styles of communication, less on drinking.	No control group; after one year of treatment improvements in interactions, 2 men abstinent and 3 drinking less
Gacic[70]	50 men, & wives, & children where possible	Out-patient; preparatory phase of 1-100 sessions, then 2 months intensive daily, then stabilisation period of weekly treatment for a year or more; supplemented by groups involving friends, extended family and employers	Results compared with those for a similar group given 'traditional' treatment 6 years earlier; at one year 78% abstinence (vs 38% of comparison group), 90% improved marital functioning (vs 38%); results sustained at 5 years (but comparison group not followed up); ratings of outcome possibly biased? [3]

	Clients	Treatment	Outcome

(d) *Ecological Family Treatment*

Clients	Treatment	Outcome
Pattison [71]	7 lower-class multi-problem families	Public Health nurses assisted in childcare and management, marital counselling, referral to agencies for legal and financial problems	No control group; 5 families completed 15 months of treatment; improvements in marital harmony, social functioning and alcohol intake for 4 families
Davis & Hagood [72]	48 mothers with drinking problems (half single parents with young children)	Specially trained para-professional 'family rehabilitation co-ordinators' gave 6 weeks treatment to all in household following hospitalisation of mother; behavioural task-oriented approach focussing on household management, care and discipline of children, referral to welfare agencies where appropriate, discussion of interpersonal problems	No control group; follow-up on first 36 treated; improvements in drinking, family communication and household management in 23/36
Hunt & Azrin [73]	8 men with drinking problems (5 married, not all with families)	Community reinforce-ment approach based on operant model aiming to increase vocational social, recreational and family satisfactions focussing on job-seeking, financial	Matched control group; 6 months follow-up; treated group signifi-cantly more time with families, drank less, less time in hospital, found better jobs, earning twice as much, better marital satis-faction, no separations

Clients	Treatment	Outcome

(d) Ecological Family Treatment (Continued)

| | and legal help, behavioural marital help, and building up 'synthetic families' of employers, relatives clergy etc where no natural family existed. | (vs 2 in control groups) |

(e) Individual Advice or Treatment for Relatives

| Pattison et al [74] | lower-middle or working class wives | Diagnostic-therapeutic intake groups involving classes for 2-6 weeks; not psychotherapeutic; giving information, availability of community resources, introduction to Al-Anon | No control groups; most wives attended only one session and very few referred themselves to Al-Anon |
| Cohen & Krause [75] | 298 men & wives | Half 'experimental' focussing on alcohol abuse as primary disorder; half to 'traditional' family case work focussing on alcohol as a symptom for other problems in individual or family | 111/146 assigned to experimental received treatment, and 74 were followed up; after 17 months of treatment more drinking improvement in experimental (63% vs 38% in traditional) but no difference for wives or marriages; compared with the smaller non-randomly assigned untreated group, the experimental and traditional no better in marital outcome and more separated (30% vs 4%) |

First, group treatment for wives, running concurrently with treatment for their problem drinking husbands, was the subject of research in the 1950s and 1960s but has not been since then. The two better evaluated projects (the North Carolina and Edinburgh studies already referred to) report positive results, but investigators found that only a proportion of spouses, sometimes quite a small proportion, agreed to participate.

Second, conjoint group treatment, involving several couples simultaneously, has received more research attention than any other method, and two of the projects reported were quite well evaluated (those by Corder et al[64] and by Cadogan[65]). The main focus in these projects has been uniformly on marital conflict, problem solving, interactional behaviour, and communication, rather than upon drinking. Indeed, in at least two cases[63][67] the focus was explicitly taken off excessive drinking. The structure of conjoint treatment has varied however, from Cadogan's[65] once weekly open out-patient groups, to Corder et al's[64] intensive four-day conjoint treatment at the end of a month of treatment for the 'problem drinkers', and Steinglass et al's[67] intensive research and treatment programme involving conjoint hospital admission. On the whole the authors of these conjoint studies were more successful in involving some husbands of women with drinking problems, and the evidence for the value of conjoint treatment must be considered quite positive. On the other hand it is probably going too far to say, as Gallant et al[66] did, that conjoint treatment is, 'the treatment of choice'.

Third, there has been a disappointing dearth of studies of family therapy (ie family members treated with their own family rather than separately, but not treated jointly with other families). Each of the three studies reviewed under this heading have limitations, either because of the very small numbers and inconclusive results, or in the case of Gacic's[70] study from Belgrade, the difficulty of obtaining full details, and the unusual intensity of the treatment programme which makes its routine application extremely unlikely.

Fourth, Harwin[3] defined a group of treatment programmes which she termed 'ecological'. These have been aimed at a rather different target group including 'multi-problem families', single parent families with young children, and in the case of the best evaluated of these programmes (Hunt & Azrin[73]), some single men for whom one aim was to build up 'synthetic families'. They have also taken a very different approach to family treatment, focussing much less on family interaction than is the case with conjoint and family therapy studies, and much more upon problems of child-care, household management, job-seeking, and family and legal problems. Although these programmes involved quite intensive treatment, they also show great promise.

Finally, Harwin[3], points to a very significant gap in the family treatment research that has been reported. In view of the very large numbers of family members who seek advice or assistance without, or prior to, the problem drinking member of their family seeking help, it is very disappointing that there have been so few studies of advice or treatment for spouses alone. A comprehensive service for families should surely include not only the possibility of some concurrent, conjoint, or family therapy, whether drinking, interaction and communication, or ecologically focussed, but also as a major component the possibility of help for those many family members who are living with an unresolved drinking problem in the family. A particularly sensitive account of the way in which family treatment methods can be applied to families with drinking problems was that of Kaufman & Pattison[52]. They allowed for the possibility that it may be necessary to work with a 'wet' family system for some time in order to motivate the non-drinking members to remain in treatment even if the problem drinker drops out or has not yet been involved. They also recommend a synthesis of structural, systems, behavioural, and psychodynamic approaches to family therapy, and allow that a more educational, relatively drink-focussed, approach may be in order with 'functional family systems' where affection remains relatively high, but that a greater focus on family dynamics is necessary with more disturbed families. Finally, they extend their ideas about family treatment to include those problem drinkers with little or no family contact, for whom the aim must be to help re-establish contact or to aid integration with other social groups.

Finally in this section it should be pointed out how neglected children have been. Although there has now been a certain amount of research on the circumstances in which children in families with drinking problems find themselves, and the effects that these circumstances may have, research on family treatment has not yet caught up. The barriers that stand in the way of recognising and responding to drinking problems at all are often raised higher against the involvement of spouses in treatment[76], and are raised yet higher still against children gaining access to the help and advice they may need[24]. With the exception of the Belgrade study[70] none of the family studies reviewed by Harwin[3] and Steinglass[40] included children, and although reports are beginning to appear that described ways of responding to the needs of children in families with drinking problems[77], to this writer's knowledge none has yet been the subject of serious evaluative research. Again, this is a matter to which any service, aspiring to be at all comprehensive, should give serious thought.

RECOMMENDATIONS FOR SERVICE PROVISION

1. Much more attention should be paid to the high levels of stress experienced by families with a drinking problem, and also to the role which family members can play in the continuation or successful resolution of such problems. The types of stresses experienced, and the changes of role which occur, are on the whole no different in kind from those experienced by other families in distress, but they are very often of major proportions. Children and other family members are as important as partners. This recommendation applies not only to specialist practitioners and service providers, but also to those whose work is not specially focussed on problem drinking. There is some evidence that families with drinking problems utilise general medical and social services to a greater than average extent[78].

2. It should be acknowledged that there are several different models of alcohol and the family, and people should be explicit about the model(s) with which they are operating. A combination of stress-victim and systems models is likely to be a strong contender for those involved in providing treatment.

3. The partner of an identified problem drinker should always be involved in the latter's treatment wherever possible. Special effort may have to be made to engage husbands.

4. The exact form in which families are involved is probably less important than their involvement per se, but conjoint groups have received most support from research. There are a number of different possibilities, and type of treatment should probably be matched with the particular needs of the family. Possibilities include treatment with a greater focus on drinking and a more educational style where family cohesion is relatively high; a greater focus on communication and interaction where there is greater family disturbance; and treatment with more of a focus on practical or ecological issues in the case of multiple problem families.

5. A comprehensive service should also make available counselling and advice services for partners alone when drinkers are unavailable for treatment. The balance of opinion, and what little research has been carried out on the subject, suggests that partners may be helped *to reduce* the level of their criticism of the drinker, their encouragement of his/her drinking, their enmeshment in attempts to modify the drinker to the exclusion of pursuing their own life, and their own level of guilt, and *to increase* their level of engagement with the drinker in a constructively confronting manner.

6. The considerable needs of children living in families with drinking problems have been largely neglected, and service providers should make it a priority to consider ways of responding to these neeeds.

Although one major reviewer has concluded that:

'... there is strong indication that family treatment for alcoholism can be successful... Treatment which begins with the family is apparently successful in producing change both in the alcoholic and the family'[79],

the evidence is that the larger number of agencies which provide treatment for problem drinkers do not involve partners or children, and that when they do they are rarely involved in family or conjoint treatment[80].

References

1. Hansen, D.A. & Hill, R. 'Families under Stress' in Christensen, H.T., (Ed.) *Handbook of Marriage and the Family*. Chicago, Rand McNally, 1964, 782-819.

2. Ablon, J. 'The Significance of Cultural Patterning for the 'Alcoholic Family', *Family Process*. 19, 1980, 1271-44.

3. Harwin, J. 'Alcohol, The Family and Treatment' in Orford, J. & Harwin, J. (Eds.) *Alcohol and the Family*. Croom Helm, London, 1982.

4. Shaw, S. 'Social Influences on the Use of Alcohol in the Family' in Orford, J. & Harwin, J. (Eds.) *Alcohol and the Family*. Croom Helm, London, 1982.

5. Orford, J., Oppenheimer, E., Egert, S., Hensman, C. & Guthrie, S. 'The Cohesiveness of Alcoholism - Complicated Marriages and its Influence on Treatment Outcome' *British Journal of Psychiatry*. 128, 1976, 318-339.

6. Bailey, M.B., Haberman, P., & Alksne, H. 'Outcomes of Alcoholic Marriages; Endurance, Termination or Recovery' *Quarterly Journal of Studies on Alcohol*. 23, 1962, 610-623.

7. Jackson, J.K. & Kogan, K.L. 'The Search for Solutions; Help- seeking Patterns of Families of Active and Inactive Alcoholics' *Quarterly Journal of Studies on Alcohol*. 24, 1963, 449-472.

8. Wiseman, J.P. 'The Other Half: Wife of an Alcoholic in Finland I. Early Diagnosis and Therapeutic Strategies on the Home Front' *Alkoholi Polipikka*. 41, 1976, 62-72.

9. Hayashi, S. 'Alcoholism and Marriage: Family Court Divorce Conciliation' *Japanese Journal of Studies on Alcohol*. 13, 1978, 177-190.

10. Ryle, A. 'A Marital Patterns Test for use in Psychiatric Research' *British Journal of Psychiatry*. 112, 1966, 285-293.

11. Lemert, E.M. 'Dependency in Married Alcoholics' *Quarterly Journal of Studies on Alcohol*. 23, 1962, 590-609.

12. O'Farrell, T.J., 'Marital Stability Among Wives of Alcoholics, Reported Antecedents of a wife's decision to separate from or endure an alcoholic husband' *Dissertation Abstracts International*. Vol 36, Oct, 1975.

13. Orford, J. 'Alcoholism and Marriage: The Argument Against Specialism' *Journal of Studies on Alcohol*. 36, 1975, 1537-63.

14. Gayford, J.J. 'Wife Battering: A Preliminary Study of 100 cases' *British Medical Journal.* 1, 1975, 194-197.

15. Eberle, P.A. 'Alcohol Abusers and Non-Users: A Discriminant Function Analysis of Differences between two sub-groups of Batterers' *Journal of Health and Social Behaviour.* 23, 1982, 260-271.

16. Byles, J.A. 'Violence, Alcohol Problems and Other Problems in Disintegrating Families' *Journal of Studies on Alcohol.* 39 (3), 1978, 551-553.

17. Jackson, J.K. 'The Adjustment of the Family to the Crisis of Alcoholism' *Quarterly Journal of Studies on Alcohol.* 15, 1954, 562-586.

18. Bailey, M.B. 'Psychophysiological Impairment in Wives of Alcoholics as related to the Husbands' Drinking and Sobriety' in Fox, R., (Ed.) *Alcoholism; Behavioural Research, Therapeutic Approaches.* New York, Springer, 1967, 134-144

19. Levinger, G. 'Marital Cohesiveness and Dissolution; An Integrative Review' *Journal of Marriage and the Family.* 27, 1965, 19-28.

20. Haberman, P.W. 'Some Characteristics of Alcoholic Marriages differentiated by Level of Deviance' *Journal of Marriage and the Family.* Chicago, Rand McNally, 1964.

21. Jacob, T. & Seilhamer, R.A. 'The Impact on Spouses and how they Cope' in Orford, J. & Harwin, J. (Eds.) *Alcohol and the Family.* Croom Helm, 1982.

22. Dahlgren, L. 'Female Alcoholics IV Marital Situations and Husbands' *Acta Psychiatrica Scandinavica.* 59, 1979, 59-69.

23. Cork, R.M. *The Forgotten Children: A Study of Children with Alcoholic Parents.* Alcoholism and Drug Addiction Research Foundation of Ontario, Toronto, 1969.

24. Wilson, C. 'The Impact on Children' in Orford, J. & Harwin, J. (Eds.) *Alcohol and the Family.* Croom Helm, London, 1982.

25. Wolin, S.J., Bennett, L.A. & Noonan, D.L. 'Family Rituals and the Recurrence of Alcoholism over Generations' *American Journal of Psychiatry.* 136 (4b), April, 1979, 583-593.

26. Wilson, C. & Orford, J. 'Children of Alcoholics: Report of a Preliminary Study and Comments on the Literature' *Journal of Studies on Alcohol.* 39, 1978, 121-142.

27. Keane, A. & Roche, D. 'Developmental Disorders in the Children of Male Alcoholics' *Proceedings of 20th International Institute on the Prevention and Treatment of Alcoholism.* Manchester, ICAA Lausanne, 1974.

28. Valleman, R. & Orford, J. *Adult children of Problem Drinking Parents.* Final Research Report to DHSS, 1984.

29. el-Guebaly, N. & Offord, D.R. 'The Offspring of Alcoholics: A Critical Review'. *American Journal of Psychiatry,* 134, 1977, 357-365.

30. Goodwin, D.W. *Is Alcoholism Hereditary?* Oxford University Press, New York, 1976.

31. Cotton, N.S. 'The Familial Incidence of Alcoholism: A Review' *Journal of Studies on Alcohol.* 40, 1979, 89-116.

32. Davies, J.B. 'The Transmission of Alcohol Problems in the Family' in Orford, J. & Harwin, J. (Eds.) *Alcohol and the Family.* Croom Helm, London, 1982.

33. Murray, R. & Stabenau, J. 'Genetic Factors in Alcoholism Predisposition' in Pattison, E.M. & Kaufman, E. (Eds.) *Encyclopedic Handbook of Alcoholism.* Gardner Press, New York, 1982.

34. Mishara, B.L. & Kastenbaum, R. *Alcohol and Old Age.* Grune and Stratton, New York, 1980.

35. Hunt, L. *Alcohol Related Problems.* Heinemann, London, 1982.

36. Streissguth, A.P. 'Maternal Alcoholism and the Outcome of Pregnancy: A Review of the Fetal Alcohol Syndrome' in Greenblatt, M. & Shuckit, M.A. (Eds.) *Alcohol Problems in Women and Children.* Grune and Stratton, New York, 1976.

37. Rosett, H.L. & Weiner, L. 'Effects of Alcohol on the Fetus' in Greenblatt, M. & Shuckit, M.A. (Eds.) *Alcohol Problems in Women and Children.* Grune and Stratton, New York, 1976.

38. Kogan, K.L. & Jackson, J.K. 'Some Concomitants of Personal Difficulties in Wives of Alcoholics and Non-Alcoholics' *Quarterly Journal of Studies on Alcohol.* 26, 1965, 595-604.

39. Kaufman, E. 'Myth and Reality in the Family Patterns and Treatment of Substance Abusers' *American Journal of Drug and Alcohol Abuse.* 7, 1980, 257-279.

40. Steinglass, P. 'Experimenting with Family Treatment Approaches to Alcoholism, 1950-1975: A Review' *Family Process.* 15, 1976, 97-123.

41. Paolino, T.J. & McCrady, B.S. *The Alcoholic Marriage: Alternative Perspectives.* Grune and Stratton, New York, 1977.

42. Stanton, M.D. 'Family Treatment Approaches to Drug Abuse Problems: A Review' *Family Process.* 18, 1979, 251-280.

43. Steinglass, P. 'The Roles of Alcohol in Family Systems' in Orford, J. & Harwin, J. (Eds.) *Alcohol and the Family.* Croom Helm, London, 1982.

44. Gorad, S.L. 'Communicational Styles and Interaction of Alcoholics and their Wives' *Family Process.* 10, 1971, 475-489.

45. McCrady, B.S. 'Marital Dysfunction: Alcoholism and Marriage' in Orford, J. & Harwin, J. (Eds.) *Alcohol and the Family.* Croom Helm, London, 1982.

46. Hersen, M., Miller, P. & Eisler, R. 'Interactions between Alcoholics and their Wives; A Descriptive Analysis of Verbal and Non-Verbal Behaviour' *Quarterly Journal of Studies on Alcohol.* 34, 1973, 516-520.

47. Becker, J.V. & Miller, P.M. 'Verbal and Non-Verbal Marital Interaction Patterns of Alcoholics and Non-Alcoholics' *Journal of Studies on Alcohol.* 37, 1976, 1616-24.

48. Jacob, T., Ritchey, D., Cvitkovic, J.F. & Blane, H.T. 'Communication Styles of Alcoholic and Non-Alcoholic Families when Drinking and Not Drinking' *Journal of Studies on Alcohol.* 42, 1981, 466-482.

49. Billings, A.G., Kessler, M., Gonberg, C.A. & Weiner, S. 'Marital Conflict Resolution of Alcoholic and Non-Alcoholic Couples during Drinking and Non-Drinking Sessions' *Journal of Studies on Alcohol.* 40, 1979, 183-195.

50. Drewery, J. & Rae, J.B. 'A Group Comparison of Alcoholic and Non-Alcoholic Marriages using the Interpersonal Perception Technique' *British Journal of Psychiatry.* 115, 1969, 287-300.

51. Chiles, J.A., Stauss, F.S. & Benjamin, L.S. 'Marital Conflict and Sexual Dysfunction in Alcoholic and Non-Alcoholic Couples' *British Journal of Psychiatry.* 137, 1980, 266-273.

52. Kaufman, E. & Pattison, E.M. 'Differential Methods of Family Therapy in the Treatment of Alcoholism' *Journal of Studies on Alcohol.* 42, 1981, 951-971.

53. Wilson, C. *Interactions in Families with Alcohol Problems.* Unpublished M. Phil. Dissertation, University of London, 1983.

54. Orford, J., Guthrie, S., Nicholls, P., Oppenheimer, E., Egert, S. & Hensman, C. 'Self-Reported Coping Behaviour of Wives of Alcoholics and its Associations with Drinking Outcome' *Journal of Studies on Alcohol.* 36, 1975, 1254-67.

55. Schaffer, J.B. & Tyler, J.D. 'Degree of Sobriety in Male Alcoholics and Coping Styles Used by their Wives' *British Journal of Psychiatry.* 135, 1979, 431-437.

56. Meyer, M. *Drinking Problems Equal Family Problems: Practical Guidelines for the Problem Drinker, the Partner and all those Involved.* Lancaster, Momenta, 1982.

57. Seixas, J. *How to Cope with an Alcoholic Parent.* Edinburgh, Canongate, 1980.

58. Gorman, J.M. & Rooney, J.F. 'The Influence of Al-Anon on the Coping Behaviour of Wives of Alcoholics' *Journal of Studies on Alcohol.* 40(11), 1979, 1030-38.

59. Ewing, J.A., Long, V. & Wenzel, G.G. 'Concurrent Group Psychotherapy of Alcoholic Patients and their Wives' *International Journal of Group Psychotherapy.* 11, 3, 1961, 329-338.

60. Smith, C.G. 'Alcoholics: their Treatment and their Wives' *British Journal of Psychiatry.* 115, 1969, 1039-42.

61. Bromet, E. & Moos, R.H. 'Environmental Resources and the Post- treatment Functioning of Alcoholic Patients' *Journal of Health and Social Behaviour.* 18, 1977, 326-338.

62. Gliedman, L.H., Rosenthal, D., Frank, J.D. & Nash, H.T. 'Group Therapy of Alcoholics with Concurrent Group Meetings of their Wives' *Quarterly Journal of Studies on Alcohol.* 17, 1956, 655-670.

63. Burton, G. & Kaplan, H.M. 'Group Counselling in Conflicted Marriages where Alcoholism is Present: Clients' Evaluation of Effectiveness' *Journal of Marriage and the Family.* 30, 1968a, 74-79.

64. Corder, B.F., Corder, R.F. & Laidlaw, N.D. 'An Intensive Treatment Program for Alcoholics and their Wives' *Quarterly Journal of Studies on Alcohol.* 33, 1972, 1144-46.

65. Cadogan, D.A. 'Marital Group Therapy in the Treatment of Alcoholism' *Quarterly Journal of Studies on Alcohol.* 34, 1973, 1187-94.

66. Gallant, D.M., Rich, A., Bey, E., & Terranova, L. 'Group Psychotherapy with Married Couples: A Successful Technique in New Orleans Alcoholism Clinic Patients' *Journal of the Louisana State Medical Society.* 1970.

67. Steinglass, P. 'An Experimental Treatment Program for Alcoholic Couples' *Journal of Studies on Alcohol.* 40(3), 1979, 149-182.

68. Jedberg, A.G. & Campbell, L. 'A Comparison of Four Behavioural Treatments of Alcoholism' *Journal of Behaviour Therapy and Experimental Psychiatry.* 5, 1974, 251-256.

69. Meeks, D.E. & Kelly, C. 'Family Therapy with the Families of Recovering Alcoholics' *Quarterly Journal of Studies on Alcohol.* 31, 1970, 339-413.

70. Gacic, B. *Experiences in Evaluation of the Family Therapy of Alcoholism - the Institute for Mental Health in Belgrade.* Paper presented at 26th International Institute on the Prevention and Treatment of Alcoholism, Cardiff, 1980.

71. Pattison, E.M. 'Treatment of Alcoholic Families with Nurse Home Visits' *Family Process.* 4, 1, 1965, 75-94.

72. Davis, T.S. & Hagood, L. 'In-home Support for Recovering Alcoholic Mothers and their Families: the Family Rehabilitation Co-ordination Project' *Journal of Studies on Alcohol.* 40, 3, 1979, 313-317.

73. Hunt, G.M. & Azrin, N.H. 'A Community Reinforcement Approach to Alcoholism' *Behaviour Research and Therapy.* 11, 1973, 91-104.

74. Pattison, E.M., Courlas, P.G., Patti, R., Mann, B. & Mullen, D. 'Diagnostic-therapeutic Intake Groups for Wives of Alcoholics' *Quarterly Journal of Studies on Alcohol.* 26, 1965, 605-616.

75. Cohen, P.C. & Krause, M.D. 'Casework with the Wives of Alcoholics' *Family Service Association of America,* New York, 1971.

76. Ritson, B. 'Organisation of Services to Families of Alcoholics' in Orford, J. & Harwin, J. (Eds.) *Alcohol and the Family*. Croom Helm, London, 1982.

77. U.S. National Institute on Alcohol Abuse and Alcoholism. *Services for Children of Alcoholics*. Symposium held on 24-6 September, Silver Springs, Maryland (Res. Mon. No. 4, DHHS Publication No. ADM 81-1007), U.S. Government Printing Office, Washington D.C.

78. Roberts, K.S. & Brent, E.E. 'Physician Utilisation and Illness Patterns in Families of Alcoholics' *Journal of Studies on Alcohol*. 43, 1982, 119-128.

79. Janzen, C. 'Families in the Treatment of Alcoholism' *Journal of Studies on Alcohol*. 38, 1977, 114-130.

80. Regan, J.M., Connors, G.J., O'Farrell, T.J & Jones, W.C. 'Services for the Families of Alcoholics: A Survey of Treatment Agencies in Massachusetts' *Journal of Studies on Alcohol*. 44, 1983, 1072-82.

Addiction: An Everyday 'Disease'

Rowdy Yates

The history of British policy and legislation on addiction is an extraordinary tangle of compromise between conflicting opinions and interests (see McLean in this volume). Berridge [1] has shown how the way in which legislation was formulated in the early years of the century was essentially a result of the rivalry between the Home Office and the then newly established Ministry of Health for control of the treatment and legislative response mechanisms to drug-use. The report of the Advisory Council on the Misuse of Drugs Treatment and Rehabilitation [2] provides us with a more recent example of this process. Although the report is clearly a radical move away from the outmoded disease-model of addiction, the implications of its recommendations are to extend the power and control of the specialist drug treatment units (the 'clinics') whilst concurrently restricting the role of general practitioners.

Unfortunately the effect of this process is to enhance the aura of mystique and hysteria which surrounds addiction. If addiction is seen as a rare and exotic phenomenon which can be managed and treated only by specialist experts, this perception increases the feelings of impotence amongst non-specialist practitioners and can lead to the effective withdrawal of a range of generic services, for example, housing, primary health care, work-experience schemes, for a client group in grave need of resources. Indeed there is evidence[3] that this is becoming increasingly so. Strang[3] recently argued that as the drug-subculture expands it begins to encompass individuals whose lifestyles and behaviour are remarkably 'normal'. If this is the case then our efforts should be directed more towards assuring the involvement of non-specialist practitioners than to undermining their self-confidence and credibility. To achieve this aim requires the development and vigorous promotion of straightforward treatment and intervention strategies which, whilst not ignoring the continuing debate regarding the nature and diversity of addictive behaviour, are not hampered by it in their practical application.

Perhaps the most damaging effect of the promotion of addiction as a strange and highly specialised emotional/biological disorder is the assumption that it is therefore a single, identifiable phenomenon. In practice, use of drugs and its implications for the user are as varied as the individuals involved. Drug-use can be crudely divided into three basic categories[4][5]:

a)*Experimental* where the selection of drug-type is often indiscriminate as is the choice of setting. Incidence will generally be spontaneous and therefore often spasmodic or infrequent.

b)*Recreational* where the selection of drug-type is usually more discriminate. Usage will generally form a response to a specific set of situational cues, such as immediate setting, time, company, financial resources.

c)*Dependent* where drugs are consumed regularly with scant regard for the appropriateness of the situation. Dependent drug-use is often a singular activity carried out in isolation where decisions regarding quality of experience and drug-type are increasingly less important.

Thus, most young people will experiment with alcohol in their mid-teens. The incidence of drunkenness within this age group is significantly higher than in any other since the ability to control and channel the effect has not yet been learnt[6][7]. The majority will go on to become recreational (or 'social') drinkers. By this stage the process will have become more selective with alcohol type usually restricted to two or three particular drinks. Recreational drinkers will often discriminate between different drinking places and even brand names. They will also have learnt to distinguish between appropriate and inappropriate situations. Thus the recreational drinker will recognise the inadvisability of excessive intoxication during a business lunch whilst she/he might consider such behaviour acceptable in other situations. Some recreational drinkers or even experimenters may move into a more dependent phase of drinking. For some this may be a short-term change in response to a specific problem such as the loss of a spouse, redundancy, or pressure of work. For others the change may appear more permanent with the original cues becoming compounded and reinforced by continued drinking.

However, the three basic categories do not represent a structure through which drug-users will inevitably progress. With many drugs, the majority will experiment for only a short time before changing or reverting to a more personally satisfying activity. Even dependent usage is unlikely to prove the irreversible condition we often assume. Stimson, Oppenheimer and Thorley[8] surveyed a large group of heroin-users attending drug-treatment units in

London and in a seven-year follow-up almost one third were found to be no longer physically dependent. Since there is also evidence[9][10] that those attending such clinics are often particularly problematic drug-users for whom prognosis is normally poor, it might be assumed that the actual self-recovery rate is significantly better than even this study would suggest, and there are a number of other studies [11][12][13] which also support Stimson's findings.

The importance of separating drug-use into the three categories lies in the implications for selecting the appropriate treatment response. Thus the fifteen year-old who is experimenting with a variety of substances is unlikely to benefit from long-term therapy in a residential rehabilitation hostel. Similarly, the dependent heroin-user of ten years standing is likely to take a fairly dim view of a stern lecture on the dangers of that particular drug. Clearly the appropriate treatment response depends upon an accurate assessment of the nature and implications of drug taking in each individual case. Failure to employ such criteria will almost certainly lead to an ineffective and occasionally counter-productive intervention.

The aim of any constructive intervention is to identify and resolve two distinct and separate sets of problems:

Primary Problems - which stem directly from the nature of the drug being used, the mode of application, and societal and familial responses. Thus the user of an illegal drug will almost certainly have problems with the law; injectors run the risk of contracting hepatitis; and users of heavy intoxicants will face problems in operating complex machinery (eg. drinking and driving).

Secondary Problems - some, though by no means all, drug-users may also present in treatment with a second series of problems which do not arise out of their drug-use but are problems to which drug-taking was originally, or has become, a response. Thus, those who believe themselves to be in some way inadequate may well find comfort and solace in drug-use. The use of minor tranquillisers can mask dissatisfaction with an unrewarding marriage or frustration with an inability to cope with the demands of work or parenthood.

This breakdown is not, of course, simply related to drug-use but is apparent in every activity we indulge in to alter our mood. Every experience which radically changes the way we feel has a capacity to draw us back into its comforting embrace; to become a habit whether good, bad or indifferent.

'Drug addiction' is little more than a specialised term for a habit which has gone out of control and which is generally regarded by society and often by the drug-user him/herself as bad. Peele [14][15] suggests that addiction can be more readily understood when it is seen, not as a pathological condition, but rather as an uncontrolled behaviour which lies at the end of a spectrum or continuum of normal behaviour. The aim in treatment then is to identify the degree to which drug-use is a significant factor in an individual's life and the problems to which such an activity provides a solution, however transitory.

In exploring the problems which might lie between an individual's use of drugs, or which might result from it, the following model may prove useful as a mental note to clarify the issues both for the doctor/therapist and for the customer or drug-user[16]:

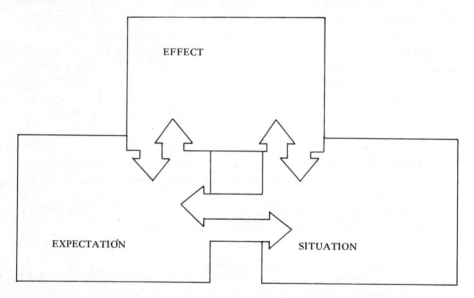

The model assumes three interacting factors in the use of drugs or any other mood-changing experience. Determining the relative importance of each factor to an individual's pattern of drug-use should lead to a logical assessment of the appropriate treatment response.

Effect [17]

It is clearly not possible to become dependent upon an experience which does not have the capacity to change the feelings or mood of the user. Radical alteration of mood may cause problems for the user in terms of impaired ability.

In cases of heavy intoxication, accidents or even non-deliberate overdose may result. Clearly the toxic effects of some, though by no means all, substances and/or the means of application can constitute a serious health risk. Moreover, some drug-users may continue the activity simply through a fear of the after-effects of 'withdrawal'.

Addiction is not a search for 'kicks' but a retreat into a comfortingly predictable experience. Logically, therefore, recreational or controlled drug-use is likely to be marked by an emphasis on the 'quality' of the experience, and the recreational drinker will make a series of decisions in embarking upon the chosen course. What type of drink? What drinking place? Who with? Conversely the alcoholic according to the degree of dependence, will find his/her choices progressively limited. The alcoholic who happens to have a fancy for single-malt whiskey is thus unlikely to refrain from drinking if such a commodity is for some reason unavailable. Addiction is an indiscriminate process. Many specialist practitioners[18] have noted a progressive decrease in selectivity with some individuals, often characterised by a drift away from 'glamorous' drug-use (heroin and the opiates) towards the more mundane end of the market (alcohol, valium and anything that is easily accessible).

Situation [19]

Many people will use drugs in response to a particular situation; or the way in which they use may change to reflect an altered circumstance. For instance, almost one-third of all U.S. troops in Vietnam were believed to be heavily addicted to heroin. Alarming predictions were made about the probability of an explosion of heroin addiction in America when and if those troops were returned home but the explosion never happened. Robins[11] found only 7% became readdicted after they had been flown home. Indeed one of the surprising findings was that many of those who continued to use heroin did so in a recreational way and appeared to have achieved a large measure of control over their habit.

The reasons are not hard to find. Whilst in Vietnam, young Americans found themselves directly involved in a war for which there was mixed support at home. They were separated from the influences which would normally exercise some control over their behaviour such as family, work, academic career, and the antipathy of American society towards heroin use. Most important of all, they found themselves in a situation where heroin was readily available and where they were in real and continual danger. Perhaps in such a situation heroin begins to look like a rational solution, at least for as long as that situation lasts.

Where situation is a significant factor there may well be an indentifiable 'pay-off' to using drugs. It may even be regarded as an occupational hazard (eg. the use of amphetamines by long-distance lorry drivers). Alternatively the phenomenon might be a group response to frustration and boredom and will probably continue in some form until more interesting/exciting/rewarding activities can be found, or for as long as the group or individuals within it are unable to perceive such alternative options. In such cases actual changes in the situation, e.g. falling in love, obtaining employment, removal from the war-zone, can precipitate dramatic changes in an individual's use of drugs. Many people continue to use drugs for years simply because they do not know of or do not understand the alternative options/strategies.

Expectation [20] [21]

The experience of drugs is largely conditioned by expectations. Various experiments with inert substances or placebos[22] have shown that an individual's belief in the efficacy of a treatment regime can override even acute pain. In one classic study Lasagna[23] found that 30-40% of patients could not tell the difference between morphine and a placebo when these were administered for severe post operative pain.

We can take this argument a stage further and suggest that not only the physical effects of drugs but also the way in which we use and experience them are strongly influenced by the beliefs and expectations of the society in which we happen to live. Inglis[24] has described in detail the way in which opium has been regarded in different ways by different cultures, sometimes as a depressant, sometimes as a stimulant and occasionally (as in Victorian England) as a hallucinogenic. Similarly, tobacco was originally used by native American Indians as a hallucinatory substance, yet no such usage has been recorded in this country.

Furthermore there is a wealth of evidence that where drugs are adopted by, or imposed upon, cultures, the impact in terms of social and personal disruption is far greater than in those countries where their usage is part of the traditional fabric. Marais[25] has described the devastating effects of tobacco on the Hottentot society of nineteenth-century Africa. Yet the use of marijuana amongst these people had been accepted and commonplace for generations. The introduction of alcohol to native American Indians is known to have had similarly disastrous effects. Again, Inglis[24] records how the smoking of opium in the Indian sub-continent, where this was a commonplace practice of long-standing, was not associated with any serious social or moral decline. Yet its imposition by British warlords upon the Chinese caused untold damage.

It is clear therefore that where a substance is relatively unknown and where it is accompanied by a backlash of moral indignation and panic, its actual effect becomes severely distorted through the manipulation of the expectations of prospective users.

However, expectation is not simply a belief in the power and effect of specific substances. It also encompasses personal value systems about how you see yourself; your belief (or lack of it) in your own ability to cope with certain situations and your perspective on what life might hold in store for you. Thus an individual's involvement with, and continuation in, destructive patterns of drug-use is often related to his/her lack of self-belief and to the failure to comprehend his/her own power to change or control a situation. It follows that any intervention or treatment model geared towards achieving abstinence will founder if it fails to offer alternative strategies which serve to re-adjust the level of self-belief and esteem. Conversely, any response which underlines and condones the drug-user's patient or victim/inadequate role will automatically reinforce the addictive behaviour.

Assessment models of the type outlined above are useful in developing an approach to addiction treatment which has a rational problem-solving base. This approach, whilst it does not ignore the complexities of drug-using behaviour, places it in perspective by analysing its relationship to the difficulties which stem from it and/or those to which it has become a response. Thus a constructive intervention would begin with a careful assessment of the relative importance of each of the three factors:

Effect

Do you use more than one type of drug?
Are there any particular drugs you would not use?
How do they make you feel?
Have you ever achieved this feeling in other ways?
Did you ever attempt to stop - how did that feel?

Situation

Do you have any friends who do not use?
Have any of your friends stopped - what happened to them?
What are your prospects in terms of employment, relationships, housing etc.?

98

Are you and/or your friends interested or involved in any other activities? Is your usage regular or is it restricted to specific times and places?

Expectation

How would you describe yourself?
How do you think other people see you?
How do you feel about the differences between these two pictures?
What would be the perfect picture and what would you have to do to achieve this?
What do you believe might happen to you if you stop using drugs?

The use of such a model does not preclude consideration of the physical components of addictive behaviour. Nor is it to deny their existence or importance. Rather it is to recognise that a complicated interaction of physical and psychological factors is in operation, a process about which we know little and understand less. We know, for instance, that stomach ulcers have a psychological, stress-related component. This does not mean that they are 'all in the mind'. They can be seen on an X-ray. And they hurt! The remedy however lies not simply in a physical cure. It is also important to identify social and emotional strategies which can minimise the pain and, more importantly, prevent re-occurrence.

The prevention of re-occurrence or re-addiction is a crucial question (see Saunders in this volume). To leave behind a comforting, reassuring behaviour and enter a more threatening existence is a hazardous move which most individuals will take slowly and may well not achieve at the first attempt. Marlatt[26] has shown that most relapses are preceded by a small (and objectively unimportant) lapse which undermines the self-belief of the individual as an 'abstainer'. If these findings are correct, then specialist treatment units with their emphasis on abstinence as the only worthwhile and meaningful goal have a great deal to answer for.

Experience with tobacco suggests that most individuals achieve abstinence not in a single quantum leap, powered by that elusive beast 'motivation', but that the majority of those who successfully abstain do so at the tag-end of a number of unsuccessful attempts (again see Saunders in this volume). Just like riding a bicycle, the process of changing a behaviour pattern through which abstinence is achieved is a skill which must be learnt. Falling off a bicycle does not mean that you are never going to be able to ride one. The drug-using customer should be discouraged from seeing every lapse as a relapse and encouraged to use the experience to learn new strategies for overcoming particular difficulties and situations.

The view of the drug addict as an exotic and incurable sufferer from a mysterious disease has underlined the formation of British policy and legislation throughout the twentieth century. It has been responsible for a series of draconian edicts on the statute book. The influence of such legislation coupled with the extraordinary power of the 'yellow' press (see Asquith in this volume) has encouraged even more strident, even more hysterical public opinion. The attitudes involved appear to be based more on an atavistic belief in possession by devils than a rational assessment of the actual nature of addictive behaviour.

With a rapidly expanding blackmarket in imported opiates, continuing high levels of unemployment and a lamentably inadequate specialist treatment system, the task which faces society in Britain is not one of ever increasing containment and law enforcement but one which demands a radical re-alignment of our current beliefs. It we are to come to terms with the management and control of addiction we will have to put on one side the current popular view of drug-taking.

Until we can begin to see addiction as an extension of normal, and thus reversible, behaviour it must inevitably remain the 'untreatable' preserve of a specialist elite. Until we can adopt a more pragmatic approach which encourages the involvement of the generic services, the 'drug problem' must remain within the shadowy pigeonhole to which we have consigned it; a menacing and dangerous disease which can be produced on occasion as an ogre to frighten young children; a symbol of the immorality of youth; and a degenerate spectacle with which to titillate the masses.

In 1963 Trocchi[27] wrote scathingly of the unhelpful and misinformed way in which addiction is viewed. Sadly little has changed to contradict his depressingly sharp insight:

'It's a nice tangible cause for juvenile delinquency. And it lets most people out because they're alcoholics. There's an available pool of wasted looking bastards to stand trial as corrupters of their children. It provides the police with something to do, and as junkies and pot-heads are relatively easy to apprehend because they have to take so many chances to get hold of their drugs, a heroic police can make spectacular arrests, lawyers can do a brisk business, judges can make speeches, the big peddlers can make fortunes, the tabloids can sell millions of copies. John Citizen can sit back and watch evil get its just desserts.'

References

1. Berridge, V. 'Drugs and Social Policy: the Establishment of Drug Control in Britain 1900-1930' *British Journal of Addiction*. (Centenary Edition) London, 1984.

2. Advisory Council on Misuse of Drugs. *Treatment and Rehabilitation*. H.M.S.O. London, 1982.

3. Strang, J. 'Problem Drug-Taking' *Medicine International*. Oxford, October, 1984.

4. Kay, L. *A United Kingdom Perspective on Prevention of Problem Drug Use*. 8th World Conference of Therapeutic Communities, Rome, 1984.

5. Kay, L. 'What is Solvent Abuse?' *Concern* No. 48. National Children's Bureau, London, 1983.

6. *Report of the Departmental Committee on Scottish Licensing Law*. H.M.S.O. Edinburgh, 1973.

7. Flint, R. *Teenage Drinking: A Cause for Concern*. Social Work Department, Lothian Region, 1974.

8. Stimson, G.V., Oppenheimer, E. & Thorley, A. 'Seven Year Follow-up of Heroin Addicts: Drug Use and Outcome' *British Medical Journal*, May, 1978.

9. Blumberg, H.M. 'British Users of Opiate Type Drugs: A Follow-up Study' *British Journal of Addiction*. 71 (1) 1976.

10. Lukoff, I.F. *Some Aspects of the Epidemiology of Heroin Use in a Ghetto Community*. Unpublished MSS, University of Columbia, New York, 1973.

11. Robins, L. *The Vietnam Drug User Returns*. U.S. Government Printing Office, Washington, 1974

12. Zinberg, N.E. 'G.I.'s and O.J.'s in Vietnam' *New York Times*.[37] December, 1971.

13. Winick, C. 'Maturing out of Narcotic Addiction' *Bulletin on Narcotics*. 14, New York, 1962.

14. Peele, S. *How Much is Too Much?* Prentice-Hall, New Jersey, 1981.

15. Peele, S. & Brodsky, A. *Love and Addiction*. Tatlinger, New York, 1975.

16. Yates, R. *An Abstract on Addiction* CURR Public Policy Paper, University of Glasgow, 1982.

17. See also Peele, S. *Re-defining Addiction*. 3rd Annual Summer Institute of Drug Dependence, Colorado Springs, 1979.

18. Although this drift is regarded as common knowledge in practice I am not aware of the observations having been written up.

19. See also Jaffe, J. 'As Far as Heroin is Concerned, the Worst is Over' *Psychology Today*. August, 1973.

20. See Lindesmith, A.R. *Addiction and Opiates*. Aldine, Chicago, 1968.

21. See also Becker, H. *Outsiders*. Free Press of Glencoe, London, 1963.

22. Shapiro, A.K. 'Placebo effects in medicine, psychotherapy and psychoanalysis in Bergin, A.E. & Garfield, S.L. (Eds.) *Handbook of Psychotherapy and Behaviour Change*. Wiley, New York, 1971.

23. Lasagna, L. 'A Study of Placebo Response' *American Journal of Medicine*. (16) 1954.

24. Inglis, B. *The Forbidden Game*. Hodder & Stoughton, London, 1975.

25. Marais, E. *The Soul of the Ape*. Atheneum, New York, 1969.

26. Marlatt, A. Unpublished Review in *Psychology Today*. February, 1982.

27. Trocchi, A. *Cain's Book*. Calder, London, 1960.

Additional Bibliography

Edwards, G. & Busch, G. (Eds.) *Drug Problems in Britain: A Review of Ten Years*. Academic Press, London, 1981.

Stimson, G.V. & Oppenheimer, E. *Heroin Addiction: Treatment and Control in Britain*. Tavistock, London and New York, 1982.

Glue Sniffing - Politics of Certainty

Stewart Asquith and Elizabeth Jagger

INTRODUCTION

The premises on which this paper is based are that

(i) attempts to control solvent abuse are explicitly political exercises and
(ii) that the language in which solvent abuse is written about (e.g. in official policy documents, reports, texts) and spoken about (e.g. by officials, social workers) is a powerful mechanism in realising political ends. This is so for a number of reasons.

Firstly, the language of official policy statements has an important political function to play in constituting solvent abuse as a particular kind of problem, in constituting specific forms of knowledge as a legitimate basis for strategies of control and thereby in conveying certainty about the nature of the problem and the reliability of official strategies for dealing with it. That is, the language of control is a powerful political commodity whereby images of certainty are created. In referring to the symbolic significance of political language in the context of American welfare programmes Edelman[1] makes a similar point when he asserts that;

> 'In this way, the name for a problem ... creates beliefs about what conditions public policy can change and what it cannot touch' (p. 28)

and later

> 'From subtle linguistic evocations and associated governmental actions we get a great deal of our beliefs about what our problems are, their causes, their seriousness ... we are similarly cued into beliefs about which authorities can deal with which problems, and their levels of merit and competence' (p. 29).

Secondly, official policy statements may well be a poor indicator of official practice. It has become something of a sociological truism to draw the distinction between policy and practice. In this paper, our argument will be slightly different; in the context of solvent abuse, though there are important distinctions between policy statements and what is actually done, this does not mean that there is no relationship. That would be too crude a position and the empirical evidence lends little support to it. It is in this relationship that what we refer to as the politics of certainty can be more readily identified.

There is a distinct dearth of information on solvent abuse as a social practice and available research is mainly medical in orientation. (For a review of the recent publications in Britain see 'Solvent Abuse by Children and Young Adults; a Review' [2].) In the research that has been done, solvent abuse is thus discussed primarily in clinical and medical language, concentrating on the physiological effects of the practice. The use of language commonly associated with other forms of drug abuse (e.g. 'addiction', 'withdrawal symptoms', etc.) would then appear to accommodate the practice within a framework of explanation which would ultimately lead to control of the 'problem'.

However, there are two difficulties here. The first is that research has so far largely ignored the *social* implications of the practice. The second is that despite the accommodation of solvent abuse within the language of the medical experts, it is by no means clear to what use the available medical research is put by those who are charged with dealing with solvent abuse, i.e. the social worker, the policeman, or the teacher. The highly technical and quasi- scientific language in which medical research is couched may be of little relevance to those who have to deal with children who have inhaled solvents. The strategies developed by the different agencies and personnel concerned with solvent abuse constituted the focus of research conducted by Didcott and Asquith and for the purposes of this paper reference will be made to that project in order to make more general points about attempts to control the 'problem'. The main objective in this research was not to explore *what* solvent abuse is but *how* solvent abuse is conceived and the implications that these conceptions have for the policies and practices adopted by the numerous agencies and personnel concerned. The data for the project were collected in a number of ways:

(i) a number of unstructured interviews were conducted with representatives of the different agencies and groups with a direct interest in or involvement with solvent abuse - these included social workers, psychiatrists, psychologists, health officials, GPs, intermediate treatment workers, the community workers, and the police. The list reflects the diversity of interests which have a direct involvement in solvent abuse and is not without implications for how it is dealt with as we want to discuss later;

(ii) interviews were conducted with representatives from different levels within agencies;

(iii) interviews were conducted within *two* different regions in Scotland; and

(iv) the various policy statements and initiatives produced by central government and local government agencies also constituted an important source of data.

Put briefly then the research was mainly an exercise in tracing (a) the historical development of policy initiatives devised to deal with solvent abuse and (b) to examine some of the practical implications of the implementation of the strategies proposed. Again we want to repeat that we have little information on the nature of solvent abuse in terms of its social effects and cultural implications and, given that there is little information on these areas at all, this represents a significant gap in the literature and in our awareness of solvent abuse as a social practice. As we shall argue later the dearth of such knowledge is reflected in the construction of attempts to deal with the 'problem' of solvent abuse.

THE POLITICS OF CERTAINTY: OFFICIAL LANGUAGE

Since the 1960s 'helping professions' have been granted increasing responsibility for dealing with social problems - solvent abuse being a particular and most recent instance[3]. Without reviewing the arguments fully here, it is now commonplace[4] to suggest that the 'helping professions' given these increasing responsibilites, fulfil, either overtly or covertly, control functions since they form part of the ideological apparatus of the welfare state. Further, it is suggested that members of the helping professions - the social worker, community worker, child psychologist - all have considerable power to intervene in the lives of citizens by virtue of the knowledge they possess. That is, knowledge leads to power and that power is exercised as a form of control. The argument then is that despite the language of helping and caring, welfare agencies exert a subtle form of repressive coercion and the knowledge-power relationship is seen thereby to be unidirectional (knowledge leads to power) and negative (power is repressive)[4]. Our argument is that all this ignores the fact that only certain forms of knowledge are seen to be legitimate (why is social work an acceptable form of intervention?) and is based on little empirical evidence about how knowledge is deployed in the interests of control (what does the social worker do?).

In the early 1970s solvent abuse came to be seen as a real social problem and one that warranted intervention by central government. In December 1981 the

Scottish Office issued a consultative document[5] which intimated both the fact that central government was taking demands for action to combat solvent abuse seriously *and* that intervention of some form was likely. It also laid the basis on which solvent abuse is seen as essentially a welfare problem since it argued that existing arrangements with a little cooperation between existing agencies would probably offer a suitable strategy of control. In agreement with policy initiatives elsewhere the merit of multidisciplinary approach was advocated. After considerable parliamentary activity in 1982 and 1983, the Solvent Abuse (Scotland) Act[3] came into force in July 1983 making solvent abuse a ground of referral to the Children's Hearing system. Under section 32[2] of the 1983 Act, children can be referred to the Reporter on the specific ground of solvent abuse. That is, it is not an offence but a separate ground of referral in its own right. Since then there has also been the High Court decision that the sale of solvents to children with the likelihood of ensuing harm does constitute an offence and indeed the issue of *harm* has been a recurrent theme in discussions about the practice and in the advice (contained in the many and varied leaflets and articles) distributed to both professionals and the public.

As well as the issuing of central government pronouncements a proliferation of policy initiatives at local government level and from the individual agencies concerned[6] has been a hallmark of developments in recent years. In many respects, there are obviously divergent opinions about what kind of practice solvent abuse is and how to deal with it but there are also a number of points of similarity which have done much in the constitution of solvent abuse as a problematic behaviour. An analysis of these official pronouncements constructs solvent abuse in the following way.

(i) *Essentially a pathological condition*: solvent abuse is seen to be, and presented as a behavioural condition symptomatic of some underlying disturbance usually within the individual. Thus, it can be immediately seen that solvent abuse would fit very neatly into the philosophy of the Children's Hearings. But the main point is that since it is construed essentially as a pathological condition in the individual and of crucial significance, the individual is the object of intervention.

(ii) Solvent abuse is a behavioural condition subject to *professional intervention* and the agencies who have the appropriate bodies of knowledge with which to devise strategies of control are those already in existence - social work, psychiatry, child guidance etc. All the existing helping professions and the resources at their disposal therefore are constituted as the control network.

(iii) *Medical language*: of crucial significance is the employment in official statements of primarily medical or what might be referred to as paramedical language. The available research literature[7] that is utilised in the attempt to understand and explain solvent abuse and its effects is mainly medical in orientation and often based on research conducted within an industrial context (e.g. involving analyses of the effects on workers exposed to solvents of various kinds in individual processes). There is very little medical literature on the effects of solvent abuse as a social practice but what there is appears to have had considerable influence in determining what we know about the effects of solvents on users. One paper in particular[8] has been influential in fostering the belief that solvent abuse can lead to brain damage although there is disagreement in the medical profession about this and the evidence is not conclusive[9].

Now quite apart from the use of medical language the absence of alternative constructions of solvent abuse has meant that there have appeared a number of medical 'experts'. The implication is that the explanation of solvent abuse and its control are seen to focus on the body and not the person, on the medical effects and not the social effects. This is not to be taken to suggest that medical expertise and medical knowledge is not appropriate but rather that medical language is a potent force in determining our conceptions of just what it is we are dealing with. What it does is highlight the absence of information, and therefore a gap in our knowledge of the social and cultural implications of solvent abuse. Why is it so popular, what social effects does it have on the individual and his or her family? Though there is lipservice paid to the fact that there *may* be social effects (within the family, within peer groups, at school etc.) the discussion of the harm that ensues from the practice is given primarily in medical terms.

Political Functions

One of the main achievements of the language employed is the representation of official initiatives and strategies as a rational response to the problem. In effect, it not only defines the strategies but also constitutes them in the first place - in a sense the suggestions as to control proposed follow from the way the behaviour is constituted. The representation of solvent abuse as essentially a pathological problem means that it can be accommodated within an existing discourse and within a set of given institutional arrangements. What this means then is that we already have a conceptual framework for understanding, classifying, categorising and helping the child who inhales solvents. Thus, strategies of control are not accommodated to the particular requirements of the children who inhale solvents - rather the solvent abuse is conceptualised within a set of pre-existing categories and within a form of knowledge that is already legitimated.

Despite the passing of new legislation such as the 1983 Solvent Abuse Act what we have in relation to solvent abuse is basically more of the same. Cohen[10] recognises this when he says in referring to delinquency programmes that very often

> 'alternatives became not alternatives at all but new programmes which supplement the existing system or else expand it by attracting new populations'.

And since solvent abuse is not an offence it also means that the 'helping professions' are once again directly involved in the moral arena where they are dealing not with legal infractions but deviations from a norm. It is no surprise then to find that the solutions produced involve for the most part techniques directed at the adjustment or re-adjustment of the individual. Through the activities of, for example, social workers, moral conventions and social norms can be reaffirmed by the application of appropriate bodies of knowledge. Moreover, the involvement of the 'helping professions' serves to deflect attention from the fact that though the harm that children may do to themselves is *the* criterion for intervention, there are other objectives in the background. David Marshall[11], M.P. and the prime mover behind the Solvent Abuse Act, himself recognised them when he stated;

> 'Our greatest worry is that glue sniffing leads to damage to property and to the lives of innocent citizens being put at risk. Youngsters under the influence of glue are completely unaware of the effects of their actions ... (of) the horrible effects of glue sniffing'.

Thus we find contemporary expression of the difficulty of distinguishing between the deprived and the depraved, the troubled and troublesome and those who are in danger or who are dangerous.

Further the categorisation of 'solvent abuse', irrespective of the many and varied practices (in terms of extent and scale of use, type of solvents, cultural milieu) as a unidimensional phenomenon, as a behavioural category, renders it amenable to the intervention of the different agencies involved in social control. Though rendered a unidimensional category in terms of a pathological classification the child who uses solvents may nevertheless experience intervention by a number of different agencies - social work, child guidance, psychiatry, psychology, the police. What this reflects neatly is that[12]:

> 'Heterogeneous knowledges are placed in a common perspective by the formation of an extrajudicial jurisdiction made up of educators, psychologists, social assistants, psychiatrists and psychoanalysts. Their job is to draw up a synthesis and supply an extra opinion as to the most appropriate measure.'

Though Donzelet was here referring to a different historical and social context his statement is not without relevance to current attempts to deal with most deviant and delinquent behaviour in a quasi-scientific manner. The case of solvent abuse provides no better example since one of the most recent proposals, perhaps in recognising the limitations of specific agencies in dealing with the problem, is that of a 'multidisciplinary' approach or some form of 'corporate' management.

The legitimation of specific knowledge as a way of explaining, understanding and dealing with the behaviour also means that other knowledge, other ways of explaining are treated as irrelevant. Alternative scenarios are inhibited and each official pronouncement reinforces the definition of the behaviour and the categorisation framework. Thus, what children who use solvents know about solvent abuse, its attractions and effects is given little consideration. Despite official warnings in the many advice leaflets[13], they *know* that you do not die, they *know* that you do not get brain damage, they *know* you can stop if you want. Similarly, explanations of the behaviour which are given in terms of social, economic and political circumstances and the distribution of life opportunities are ignored except insofar as they are seen to explain *why* a child uses solvents. The point is that official knowledge identifies and constitutes the *individual* as the object of intervention. In relation to penal practice, Garland and Young[14] point out the way in which official language and knowledge is a powerful medium for shaping public consciousness (a view shared by Edelman[1] in the context of welfare programmes):

> 'It is in the public realm of significance, quite removed from the less visible practices of the institutions themselves that public knowledge about penal practice is primarily formed, specific problems are defined, possibilities are constructed and legitimations are offered.'

This is precisely the case we would argue with solvent abuse where, in the absence of other information, awareness of the practice is so very dependent on official images. Thus, it is not just a case of offering suggestions about how to deal with the problem but what is offered is a set of statements about what the world is like, how it can be best explained and what we should be trying to achieve. The very language, the way we speak about and write about social problems, the truth we come to hold about them are socially and politically directed. The apparatus of control and power then is not simply a repressive negative force but a productive and positive one in which the power to define leads to the legitimation of knowledge, truths and certainty. The management of a social problem like solvent abuse involves then the elimination of surprise by rendering the world eminently knowable and ultimately controllable. This is what we mean by the politics of certainty.

THE POLITICS OF CERTAINTY: OFFICIAL PRACTICE

Despite the image conveyed through the vehicle of official language, official practice in relation to the management of solvent abuse - how it is dealt with and on what premises - takes many guises. For our main study we were only able to interview members of the 'helping professions' and thus have little information on the realisation of policy through concrete practices i.e. on what the social worker, psychiatrist, doctor etc. actually do with and to 'glue sniffers'. More work needs to be done in this area since any concern with the way power is exercised in the interest of effecting change in the lives of individuals can only be identified at the point of its application. Our information abut the empirical expression of official policy depends mainly then on what people say they do and not on what they actually do. Nevertheless, even this indicates that the management of solvent abuse involves a complex set of relationships between policy and practice, and a wealth of diverse strategies and explanatory frameworks. The empirical articulation of official policy grants wide and discretionary power to a number of agencies and this manifests itself in a number of ways with important implications for the management of solvent abuse in Scotland.

Though the Solvent Abuse (Scotland) Act 1983 makes the formal referral of 'solvent users' to the Hearings system somewhat easier, at least in theory, there is no indication at all as to what should happen to such children once they are in the system. The consultative document of 1981 had suggested that existing arrangements were basically satisfactory and the 1983 Act was not premised on the commitment to innovation. Though it was accepted that something had to be done about solvent abuse, it was not clear what form intervention should take. A brief analysis of the strategies employed in Scotland reveals that what happens to a child once in the system depends less on the fact that he/she has used solvents and more on (a) geographical location (b) the agency in question and (c) the operational philosophy of specific workers within agencies. Two things can be said about the management of solvent abuse in Scotland:

(i) there is a distinct lack of agreement about what are appropriate measures to deal with solvent abuse and what the objectives of such measures should be; and

(ii) solvent abuse is the problem that no-one really wants.

We suggested earlier that medical knowledge was the dominant source of literature influencing policy statements and official attitudes[15], but the practices adopted by the different agencies and their members actually rely little on the medical knowledge available to them. It is particularly interesting that the type of knowledge employed to explain solvent abuse and inform strategies of control varied not only between the different agencies but within them. That is, though it has been suggested that solvent abuse fits neatly into a system composed of 'heterogeneous knowledges' (social work, psychiatry, psychology, etc.) the working philosophy of individual practitioners is a more important determinant of practice than membership of a particular profession. We want to illustrate this by looking at three issues

(i) The Problematic Status of Solvent Abuse

(ii) Sources of Knowledge

(iii) The Multidisciplinary Approach.

(i) *The Problematic Status of Solvent Abuse*

Is solvent abuse a problem? Before a practitioner can decide what to do about solvent abuse, he must first of all decide that it is a problem; according to those we interviewed this was not always the case. Asked whether solvent abuse was a problem, one doctor replied:

'No - kids will always find something to do - if you look at the past there have always been fads and fashions particularly associated with the young.'

The same doctor went on to say,

'There are no known long-term effects of glue sniffing'!

Recognising the cultural context, we find social workers able to say,

> 'Glue sniffing is part of the life in this area; it is very much contained and I do not think it is a problem.'

Similarly, a line offered by the Institute for the Study of Drug Dependence (ISDD) and followed by a number of practitioners is that[15];

> 'Sniffing, particularly of glue, can be a relatively harmless way of getting intoxicated, the degree of intoxication depending upon the amount taken, and is best treated similarly to teenage drinking.'

That is, the problem is the bizarre and alien nature of sniffing *for adults* although it is not necessarily any more of a problem for the young than smoking or drinking. Thus, following the casualty reduction approach advocated by the ISDD[16] a number of professionals including psychiatrists and social workers, have advocated - and employ such a tactic themselves - that glue-sniffers be taught to do it safely. The harm that results is seen to derive more from the circumstances of use rather than use per se. Certainly, over all the agencies involved in the study, there were always workers for whom the high level of concern at official levels was inappropriate and out of all proportion to the practice which could be viewed much like any other youthful or adolescent behaviour. Social workers and others then feel that they are doing no more than fulfilling a control function.

But even where solvent abuse is seen to be a problem, it is usually so only in so far as it is symptomatic of some personal need or underlying personal problem. Thus, agency workers presented with children who use solvents will endeavour to look for the 'real' problem and deal with that rather than the solvent abuse per se.

One implication of all this is that social workers, since - under the 1983 Act - they are the professionals most likely to have to work with children who sniff glue or inhale other solvents, are given responsibility for dealing with one problem (the glue sniffing) but end up dealing with another. And though there may be disagreements between social workers about what to do about it (or even whether it is a problem at all) what is constant is that it is the child or members of his family who are the objects of intervention. Even where it is recognised that social and economic circumstances may well contribute to the practice, the object of intervention is always an individual. The behaviour fits very neatly into a system of care which is based on a discourse that legitimates intervention through the individual. And, as we suggested earlier, the child who sniffs glue or uses other solvents is fitted into whatever is already available. The paradox of all this is that children referred for glue sniffing may well end up in children's homes or List D schools where glue sniffing is a real management problem. It also means that stopping children sniffing glue is not the most important criterion of successful intervention.

> 'We ran a group for hard-core glue sniffers aged 18-23 with serious problems both in and outside the glue ... at the end of 9 months, none of the kids had stopped sniffing, but that was not the intention...'

and further,

> 'We realised that there is no way we are going to change these kids in that we are never going to make them give up the glue. It is something they will do themselves.'

But if social workers, psychiatrists and others do not feel that glue sniffing as such is something they can do much about then who can be relied on to deal with it? The answer is that very often it is the police who are landed with the problem, though even they confess that it is not really a police problem.

(ii) *Sources of Knowledge*

Quite apart from the knowledge and expertise they may derive from their professional training, workers are dependent on a number of different sources of information about solvent abuse which colour their image of it. What became rather obvious was that professionals are just as susceptible to media accounts of solvent abuse and the rather sensationalist presentations contained therein. The significance of the media in informing attitudes to behaviour such as mugging has been well documented[17]. Though further analysis is needed even the media presentations are very often couched in somewhat distorted and confused medical language. In this respect also, what might be called folk myth or conventional wisdoms allow potent images of solvent abuse to be transmitted. That is, particular cases, usually of a rather dramatic nature, attain the status of apocryphal stories and are used as the basis for generalisation. The acceptance of such myths reflects both the fact that there is a distinct shortage of reliable information and that many workers may not themselves have encountered any real live cases! One worker identifies this when he states:

> 'Whatever problems are associated with solvent abuse, there is certainly one major problem - ignorance about the whole subject itself. Ignorance on the

p̄art of the sniffer himself, his parents and friends and to a large degree, on the part of the professional and other people with whom he comes into contact.'

Now this comment in its own right is rather surprising because one of the features of the management of solvent abuse has been the proliferation of advice leaflets and documents distributed to both professionals and the public in general[13]. Various institutions both within and without local authorities have produced leaflets to aid the professional in dealing with solvent abuse but they are characterised in general by two features. Firstly, such documents usually contain names and addresses of other agencies to whom the professional can refer the glue sniffer. That is, there is always another professional agency who can deal with the problem. The second feature is that while much of the information is primarily medical in nature what our interviews have revealed is that medical knowledge is a poor basis for professionals on which to base any strategy for dealing with those using solvents, for a number of reasons.

Workers are not convinced by the information that there are serious medical effects from solvent abuse and the leaflets tended to confuse rather than clarify the issue for them:

'I am still not sure what the dangers are from the health aspects: I am still dubious whether it does cause damage. I have read so many bits of paper' (Community Worker, Social Work Department),

and

'There are a lot of medical assertions about sniffing - there is very little concrete stuff - there is a lot of stuff which is elevated into scientific status. Eventually, the position is one of ignorance ... We do not know what damage it does and whether that damage is permanent or temporary.'

And even attempts to introduce workers to medical debates do not help the position;

'I came away from the (medical) seminar I attended really in a turmoil - I did not know what was right and what was wrong.'

But the medical information may not simply be difficult to comprehend but also of little relevance to the worker. When a child has been inhaling solvents and is detected while sniffing or under the influence there are no doubt good reasons at that time for conducting a medical examination (though the result is often that of allowing the effects to wear off). But the problem is very different by the time the panel member, social worker, community worker etc. is actually asked to deal with the child - this may be some weeks or even months later.

Nor is the irrelevance of a medical approach lost on members of the medical profession. A recent suggestion by the British Medical Association that glue sniffing is reaching epidemic proportions and that the medical profession should show appropriate concern is not shared by general practitioners many of whom argue that they can do little about the practice. This does not mean that they do not do anything but it does give rise to some interesting strategies.

Thus doctors have been known to have used clinical settings and tactics, such as the taking of blood samples, not for medical purposes, but with the explicit intention of intimidating and deterring children from further indulgence in the behaviour; other doctors have employed family therapy as a strategy, again after employing tactics such as these already referred to. (A curious anomaly, but one reflecting the commitment to medical knowledge, is that there have even been instances of the police introducing doctors and medical personnel to the literature on the medical effects of solvent abuse.)

The general point to be made is that there is often a conceptual gap between the knowledge employed to explain solvent abuse and its effects on the one hand and the knowledge employed on which to base appropriate strategies. There is an additional comment that can be made that the fostering of medical knowledge as the paradigm on which to base strategies may well create expectations in the public eye that the practice can be solved and that the medical profession can, quite simply, offer help to parents and children. But solvent abuse *in practice* does seem as if it is an area which the medical profession does not wish to colonise.

(iii) *Multidisciplinary Approach*

Again the bringing together of different professions with their own bodies of knowledge is seen to be the appropriate means of collating all the relevant information on a child in order to reach the right decision about what to do. However, such lofty aspirations are thwarted not simply by the fact that individual workers have to rely on their own orientations but also for other reasons. The main reason is that it is by no means clear just what form a multidisciplinary approach would take. Although the helping professions may all collect information on children, a decision still has to be made about which strategy would be most appropriate - as we have seen, there is already little consensus in that area.

A multidisciplinary approach will not mean in itself that consensus is reached and will not solve the problem of solvent abuse. Even in practical terms, different agencies may not share assumptions about the nature of the problem and what to do about it and may not even be prepared to pass on information to other agencies. Ironically, the medical profession appears most inhibited from doing so because of the issue of confidentiality.

POLITICS OF CERTAINTY: CONCLUDING REMARKS

Two aspects of the management of solvent abuse have to be distinguished - the official realm of linguistic representations and the more hidden realm of agency practices. Though the representation of solvent abuse is as the subject of specific forms of knowledge and ultimately controllable, the official practice presents a somewhat different picture. Despite the rather frenetic activity of officials at central and local government level, the management of solvent abuse is characterised by a lack of agreed practices of management. Now this may not be so surprising *between* the different agencies which in theory operate on the basis of different forms of knowledge, expertise and with different purposes in mind. But the further one goes down the hierarchy *within* agencies, then the implementation of management directives is more dependent on the working assumptions of the social worker, psychiatrist, youth worker, or psychologist. Does this mean, as we suggested earlier, that there is no relation between official policy and official practice, between linguistic representation and strategies of control? Not necessarily so. The power of official language rests, not on whether it is effective in attaining certain ends or not, but through the constitution of the problem in a particular way. In relation to solvent abuse, the significance of official statements which constitute glue sniffing as an object of professional intervention does not depend on the effects of professional strategies. Given the success of welfare programmes in dealing with delinquency that much is already apparent. The empirical data from this study revealing the diversity of strategies and techniques of management displayed in agency practices would confirm that. Again the political significance of linguistic representation is noted by Edelman[1] when, in the context of the problems of poverty and crime, he asserts:

'the names by which we refer to people and their problems continue; subtly but potently to keep attention of authorities, professionals and the general public focussed on hopes for rehabilitation of the individual and to divert attention from those results of established policies that are (actually) counterproductive',

and later,

'the result is a continuation of broad support for recurrent policies regardless of their empirical consequences'.

What Edelman has to say about poverty applies to our understanding and knowledge of many of the social problems and solvent abuse is the most recent example. Constituted as an object of knowledge and therefore of intervention, solvent abuse is fitted into an institutional framework which is already employed as the basis for intervention in the fields of delinquency, crime, and drug use generally. That is, it is yet another example of the way in which the human sciences have colonised the law and in which strategies of control are not so much concerned with legal infractions as with the adjustment or readjustment of individuals. Though there must be some doubt about the effectiveness of such strategies, what is not challenged is the set of truths on which they are based. The statements contained in official text and utterances on solvent abuse are not directed simply at managing the problem but at producing and perpetuating a body of truth, a framework for knowing the society in which we live and the problems that are taken to arise within it. Control over individuals is then not simply exercised as a repressive force but as productive. What we 'know' about the world, and from which we derive our certainty about it, is both socially and politically sustained. The management of solvent abuse is only one of the mediums through which that is achieved.

Any attempt to tackle social problems such as solvent abuse cannot simply depend on more of the same. We need to find and develop other ways of speaking and talking about them - the struggle to find these is not just linguistic, but political.

References

1. Edelman, M. *Political Language*. Academic Press, London, 1977.
2. Watson, J. 'Solvent Abuse by Children and Young Adults: A Review' *British Journal of Addictions*. 75, 1980, 27-36.
3. For example, Solvent Abuse (Scotland) Act. H.M.S.O. 1983.
4. Adler, M. & Asquith, S. (Eds.) *Discretion and Welfare*. Heinemann, London, 1981.
5. Scottish Education Department. *Consultative Memorandum on Children's Hearings and the Problem of Solvent Abuse*. 1981.

6. For example, *Solvent Abuse: A corporate approach.* Strathclyde Regional Council, 1983.

7. For a survey of this literature see Barnes, G. 'Solvent Abuse - A review' *International Journal of Addictions.* 14, 1, 1979.

8. Watson, J. 'Solvent Abuse: presentation and clinical diagnosis' *Human Toxicology.* 1, 1982, 249-256.

9. Sattaur, O. 'How glue sniffers come unstuck' *New Scientist.* 1 March, 1984.

10. Cohen, S. 'The Punitive City' *Contemporary Crises.* Vol. VIII, 1979. 339-363.

11. *Hansard.* 962 (5th Series) Cols. 433-434, 12.2.79.

12. Donzelet, J. *The Policing of Families.* Hutchinson, London, 1980.

13. See for example *Sniffing: the facts. Information for Parents* Strathclyde Regional Council, and *Sniffing: the facts. For Professional Distribution Only* also by Strathclyde Regional Council.

14. Garland, D. & Young, P. *The Power to Punish.* Heinemann, London, 1983.

15. The research that has been done so far has been primarily medical and clinical in orientation though other work has been done recently on the official response to solvent abuse (*Solvent Abuse: a study in Social Problems Theory,* by R. Peat, Pd.D. Aberdeen, unpublished).

16. Institute for the Study of Drug Dependence. *Teaching About a Volatile Situation.* Evaluation Research Unit, 1980.

17. Hall, S., Critcher, C., Jefferson, T., Clarke, J. & Roberts, B. *Policing the Crisis, Mugging, the State and Order.* Macmillan, London, 1978.

Official Responses to Drugs and Drug Dependence

Ewan MacLean

INTRODUCTION

The purpose of this paper is to outline official attitudes and policies towards the most common drugs recently and presently used in the United Kingdom, and to attempt to explain the discrepancies and contradictions which are to be found in this area. Both legal and illegal drugs will be considered, with the emphasis on heroin and the opiates, cannabis, the amphetamines and barbiturates, and alcohol and tobacco. It will be argued that U.K. drug policy and official responses, both towards physically addictive drugs and more generally towards all drugs, are fundamentally inconsistent and irrational. Drug effects and use are misunderstood, and actions are based on a confusion of different perceptions of individual and social responsibilities and rights, with intervention by central authority considered justified in some areas but not in others which are in many ways similar.

I shall also argue that, independent of pharmacological considerations, there is an underlying consistency and meaning to the differing reactions. The physical dangers inherent in the particular substances, and the personal and social harm caused by them, are not the primary reasons for the official responses to, and popular perceptions of, specific drugs. The differentiation between legal and illegal drugs is not one which can be rationally explained in terms of their chemical properties. Rather, the social position and the type of the user are of great importance. This is not to argue, of course, that many of the drugs which are presently illegal are not also in some circumstances, and when used in particular ways, both personally damaging and socially problematic, nor that all drugs are equivalent in their construction and effects.

The problems to be faced and explained are well outlined by Thorley and Plant[1];

'Complex social, legal and moral issues impinge upon the use and misuse of psychotropic drugs. There are huge and perplexing variations between national practices and gross anomalies in the legal status of certain types of drug use which have little or nothing to do with any objective assessment of the relative 'safety' or 'dangers' of any specific substance'.

In order to make my argument and analysis clear, it is first useful to outline some of the properties and effects of the most important and most used drugs, and to consider the reactions to them. Inevitably in such a short paper, many of the characteristics and complexities of even the main substances cannot be fully or adequately covered. Nevertheless, some important points can be made about them and the official policy responses which they have engendered.

HEROIN AND THE OPIATES

It seems reasonable to deal first with heroin, probably the drug most discussed and condemned in present society and which for many people is the archetypal 'drug', reputedly both addictive and deadly. Yet, such a perception is faulty and misrepresentative in a number of ways. Whilst heroin and the other opiates are certainly dependence-producing drugs - according to Kendell[2], clinical and experimental evidence suggests that taking between 20 and 30 mg. a day will lead to physical dependence within a few weeks - and whilst there appears to be a substantially higher than average mortality rate amongst present heavy users, use of the drug itself is not necessarily particularly dangerous or incapacitating. The opiates are not in fact particularly toxic, unless, as with many other substances, they are taken in large quantities. Nor is there any evidence that they produce central nervous system damage or other pathology, even after decades of continuous use. Jaffe[3] argues 'Experience with thousands of patients maintained on high daily doses of methadone (a synthetic opiate) for periods of more than 10 years has shown no direct injurious effects'. Similarly, Stimson [4], has pointed out that numerous studies show 'little evidence that pure opiates themselves cause any *direct* physical damage when administered over long periods'. He rightly continues however;

'This is not to say that many addicts do not experience physical complications, but rather that these complications are due to the manner in which the drug is administered and to the living conditions of the user rather than to the drug itself'.

In conclusion, on the long-term physical effects of the opiates, he insists that;

'Despite the high incidence of morbidity and mortality amongst addicts it must be emphasized that with a stable regular supply of the drug, with sterile injection techniques, and care of food and health, there appears to be no reason why an addict to opiates should not live out a normal life span'.

Further, as Plant[5] has argued, the seriousness of withdrawal from opiates has been often exaggerated. He notes that 'it is clear that for most users withdrawal symptoms, if they occur at all, are relatively trivial, far less serious than those involved in withdrawal from alcohol, barbiturates or certain tranquillisers'. Unfortunately, the popular mythology about the general seriousness and painfulness of withdrawal can often result in individuals refusing to attempt to fight their habits because of needless fear of the process.

Consequently, it is not specifically the drug as such or dependence on it which is the cause of most of the problems experienced by current users, but rather aspects of the surrounding personal and social environment. Unsterile and careless injections can lead to septicaemia, abcesses and hepatitis - physical disorders which do not occur when the drug is taken in other ways. One of the main reasons for this method being favoured is that it is the most efficient way of getting the drug into the body. This minimisation of waste is of importance when the substance has a high black-market cost. In countries where heroin is cheaper it is more usually inhaled, a practice which is less damaging. Further, damage and death often result from the 'cutting' of illicitly manufactured heroin with contaminants so that greater profits can be made, or through the injection of quite inappropriate substitute drugs such as barbiturates when heroin cannot be obtained. As will be argued, many legal drugs, such as alcohol and tobacco, are ultimately as physically addictive as heroin, and are in many respects in the long term significantly more damaging. But because their quality is controlled and access to them in quantity is legitimate and relatively easy and inexpensive, those dependent upon these substances generally experience fewer problems and complications than does the heroin user. Whilst accepting that heroin can be used in a dangerous or excessive way, it is therefore clear that its position in society and the reaction against it are of primary importance in the construction of both the social and individual problems presently surrounding this drug. Thus, the criminal activities which are seen to be concomitant with heroin addiction are a result not of some personal degeneracy or uninhibitedness caused by the drug, but rather arise from having to cope with the economics of the black market, whilst the degradation, suffering and death of addicts cannot simplistically be blamed on pharmacological effects.

Control of the opiates in Britain finds its origins in the late nineteenth century when the medical profession, concerned more with working-class self-medication than drug dependence, pressed for greater regulation. It was not until the second decade of this century that restriction and control became developed, and until the mid-1960s morphine and heroin could be fairly easily obtained legally through medical practitioners operating the so-called 'British System' for managing drug dependence. Until about 1960 the official attitude towards opiate addiction was low key and even unconcerned. Since the Report of the Rolleston Committee[6] of 1926, 'addiction' was seen primarily as a disease, to be controlled and treated by the medical profession (although within a penal framework which criminalised possession unauthorised by medical prescription). One of the Report's recommendations was that the provision of opiates, even if only to prevent withdrawal symptoms, was a legitimate part of medical treatment. It was also accepted that there were circumstances in which a patient might be capable of leading a useful and normal life on a regular maintenance dose of the drug, but would be incapable of doing so if this was withdrawn.

Although it was the Rolleston Committee's view that opiate addiction should in most cases be regarded as a 'manifestation of disease and not as a mere form of vicious indulgence', this was not an abstract view on dependence per se, but only on its contemporary form. The Committee continued '...the drug is taken in such cases not for the purpose of obtaining pleasure, but in order to relieve a morbid and overpowering craving'. This is an accurate perception of the type of use at that time. But there is also an implicit acceptance that the drug can be used hedonistically and non-medically, in a 'vicious' way - a practice which seems to be disapproved of, and for which the Committee had no recommendations.

For some decades after Rolleston's pronouncements there was little change in the situation. Between 1934, the first year for which figures are available, and 1963, the number of registered addicts (which can be presumed to include nearly all addicts) fluctuated between about 300 and 700. Until the early 1960s most dependence can be classified as either 'therapeutic', developed in the course of medical treatment, or 'professional', mainly that of doctors, dentists and pharmacists who developed dependence through their professional access to drugs. However, between 1958 and 1962, although the overall number of addictions was not obviously rising, there was a significant change, with an increase in the number of non-therapeutic users, mainly of heroin, who were neither as stable in their habits, or as middle-aged or middle-class as previously. The figures for such addicts known to the Home Office rose from 68 in 1958 to 212 in 1962. This development, though hardly substantial, brought about public and official anxiety and a reconsideration of the previous policy, resulting a few years later in severe tightening and controlling of the maintenance and prescription system through limiting legal provision of both heroin and cocaine to licensed doctors working in newly established clinics. Though medical involvement still remained substantial, criminal justice intervention became much more significant than previously. The Dangerous Drugs Act 1967 which contained the legislation for the new centres also brought in or extended more blatant control measures, such as Section 6 which gave police officers further powers of search to obtain evidence, and of arrest, 'in many ways in excess of all other powers given to the police'[7]. These new powers were controversial, but were defended by the police on the grounds that 'it would be extremely difficult without the new powers... to carry out the intention of Parliament to suppress drug addiction and drug peddling and to honour international agreements on drug offences'[7].

As the clinics became more organised and restricted further their provision of legal heroin, a black market began to develop to supply those who rejected, or were rejected by, the official system. As this occurred the scope for police intervention became greater, as did the number of addicts who became criminalised. Present policies can be seen to be continuing in this direction, although their lack of success is sometimes admitted by the police themselves. As Stimson and Oppenheimer[8] argue 'the new governmental analysis of the situation is... a return to a strong view of policing as the central element in the social response to drug addiction. The language of government policy no longer gives a prominent place to doctors; it is no longer they who are seen as playing a key role in controlling addiction.'

Under the Misuse of Drugs Act 1971, the main current drug-control legislation, possession of heroin or other opiates is liable to punishment of up to seven years imprisonment, whilst production or supply of these drugs carry a maximum sentence of fourteen years. The Lord Chief Justice of England and Wales, Lord Lane, recommended at the end of 1982 that large-scale importation of heroin deserved sentences of seven years and upwards, whilst 'it would seldom be that an importer of any appreciable amount would deserve less than four years'. A sentence of less than three years would seldom be justified for supplying, and for simple possession 'there would be many cases where deprivation of liberty was both appropriate and expedient'[9].

In 1983, in the whole of the United Kingdom, 1,508 persons were found guilty of offences involving heroin, 687 of whom were given custodial sentences; 379 were found guilty or cautioned for methadone offences, and 370 for dipipanone ones. Of these, 1,139 people were found guilty of unlawful possession of heroin, 282 of methadone, and 271 of dipipanone. 253 people were found guilty of unlawful supply of heroin, methadone or dipipanone, and 197 were found guilty of possession of these drugs with intent to supply[10].

Finally, the most recent official figures of known opiate addicts are, for the first time, over 10,000, whilst some sources estimate the total number of addicts in the country at over 50,000. However, as often little distinction is made between mere users and those who are really physically dependent, this latter figure has to be treated sceptically, as must recent estimates attributing some hundreds of deaths to these drugs last year. Whilst it is clear that a number of people who had been heroin users have died, the cause of their deaths, in the light of what has been argued above, cannot necessarily be connected directly to the drug. Rather, it is probable that aspects of their surrounding environment were of importance.

CANNABIS

Whilst I have argued that as a drug heroin itself is not nearly so malign as often stated, it is a powerful analgesic, the use of which, in the present circumstances, can be problematic and dangerous. The present type of consumption should therefore be discouraged, although how this can be adequately done in a way which does not create further complications and problems is not clear. Cannabis however is much more straight-forward as a drug. It is a depressant, the consumption of which usually produces a state of euphoria similar to mild alcohol intoxication.

It too is a severely controlled substance, although it is no longer included beside the opiates in the legislation. In the Misuse of Drugs Act 1971 it is classified in Class B along with the main amphetamines. Involvement with its production or supply, like heroin, carries a 14 year maximum sentence of imprisonment, whilst its possession has a maximum of 5 years. Since the late 1960s the actual sentences passed for possession have become somewhat more lenient, but offences of unlawful supply and importation are still dealt with severely. Lord Justice Lane[9] in his sentencing guidelines to the English courts suggested that possession of cannabis, when only small amounts are involved, could often be met with a fine, although, if there is 'a persistent flouting of the law, imprisonment might become necessary'. Supply of 'massive quantities' would justify sentences in the region of 10 years imprisonment, otherwise the bracket should be between one and four years, depending on the scale of operations, whilst the importation of medium quantities over 20kg. should attract sentences of three to six years imprisonment.

In 1983, for the whole of the U.K., 17,431 people were found guilty or cautioned for unlawful possession of cannabis, which was the most frequent type of drug offence, accounting for 75% of all cases; 2,535 persons were found guilty or cautioned for other cannabis offences, and 2,688 custodial sentences, the highest recorded, were given for offences involving this drug - 555 of these were for unlawful possession[10]. The previously mentioned controversial police powers of search are used extensively and mainly against cannabis users.

It is, however, not immediately clear what is so obnoxious about cannabis as to justify the fairly extensive and crude campaigns and practices against its use. It is true that Britain is a signatory to international conventions which require its control, but this is not sufficient explanation and cannot account for the magnitude of reaction against this drug. As a substance it is neither physically addictive nor obviously particularly harmful, a view confirmed by the main reports on it. In their 1968 Report on Cannabis (the 'Wootton Report'), the Advisory Committee on Drug Dependence[11] concluded;

'Having reviewed all of the material available to us we find ourselves in agreement with the conclusion reached by the Indian Hemp Drugs Commission appointed by the Government of India (1893-1894) and the New York Mayor's Committee on Marihuana (1944), that the long-term consumption of cannabis in moderate doses has no harmful effects'

and 'we think it is ... clear that, in terms of physical harmfulness, cannabis is very much less dangerous than the opiates, amphetamines and barbiturates, and also less dangerous than alcohol'.

However, according to Plant[5], cannabis cannot be considered a 'safe' drug, and even short-term consumption by smoking substantially increases the risk of lung damage and related diseases. Prolonged or heavy use may also result in some physical or psychological impairment.

But even when it is accepted that cannabis use is not usually harmful, control and action against this drug is often justified by claims that its use leads to opiate addiction since most heroin users have at some time also used cannabis. This argument contains a rather obvious logical fallacy, and such statements are merely ones of association rather than cause and effect. As Schofield[12] who was a member of the Advisory Committee argues;

'The flaw in the escalation theory is that it postulates that there is something special about cannabis. Nearly all investigations show that most heroin addicts are multiple-drug users who have tried almost anything that has come their way'.

As in all recent independent reports and investigations the Wootton Report[11] accepted that 'It can clearly be argued on the world picture that cannabis use does not lead to heroin addiction', and concluded that 'a risk of progression to heroin from cannabis is not a reason for retaining control over this drug'. Sometimes it is argued that cannabis use leads to heroin addiction through the coalescence of cannabis with heroin in illegal sub-cultures. But obviously, if this position has any validity at all, then the conclusion should be for decriminalisation of this drug, rather than the opposite. Nor is there any evidence to link cannabis use with crime.

However, it has to be acknowledged that these findings have never been generally accepted. The Wootton Report was almost completely rejected before and after its publication, and even very recently, the Scottish Health Minister[13] condemned liberalising arguments, stating that it would be much better 'if this kind of thing did not come up in public'. 'One thing leads to another', he said, and continued that 'We should be against the whole drug scene'.

THE AMPHETAMINES AND BARBITURATES

The amphetamines occupy a position somewhere between illegal drugs like heroin and cannabis, and legal ones such as alcohol and tobacco, in that there has been, especially in the recent past, both extensive licit and illicit use of them. They are stimulants which usually produce feelings of energy and confidence, effects of a moderate dose typically including increased wakefulness, improvements in concentration, reduced hunger, decreased fatigue and boredom, and an overall feeling of well-being. A similar dose may sometimes produce irritation, restlessness, nausea and confusion in some people.

Although tolerance to their various effects can develop, these drugs do not appear to be physically addictive nor does withdrawal occur if use is abruptly terminated, except probably in cases of high dosage. Nor does there 'appear to be an irreversible physiological damage associated with long-term use of moderate doses of amphetamines although temporary disorders do occur'[14]. The taking of high doses of these drugs is however more problematic and can cause 'amphetamine psychosis' and psychological dependence. Young[15] notes that,

'The effects of large doses are irritability, dizziness and tremor; very high doses may give rise to paranoid psychosis, disorientation, hallucinations, convulsions and respiratory failure'.

It should also be understood that 'speed mainlining', the intravenous injection of high doses of amphetamines or methamphetamine ('Methedrine'), is completely different from oral pill taking. Indeed, it has been argued that this form of drug-taking is more intrinsically dangerous than most. The authors of the American Consumers' Union Report[16] thought that 'the intravenous injection of large doses of amphetamines... is among the most disastrous forms of drug use yet devised' and argued further;

'The damage done by heroin... is largely traceable to antinarcotics laws and policies and to the heroin black market that has grown up under the shelter of those laws and policies... This is certainly not true of the speed phenomenon. Unlike the heroin... cases, it is large intravenous doses of the drug itself that have devastating effects in the case of speed'.

Amphetamine prescription and use was especially extensive during the 1950s and early 1960s, but was subsequently more controlled, after 'non-medical' use became apparent, by the Drugs (Prevention of Misuse) Act of 1964 which made unauthorised possession of these drugs an offence. This Act was not however concerned with legitimate medical provision, which in 1964 was responsible for almost four million prescriptions for these drugs. By 1969 amphetamines were considered to be of less medical value than previously thought, and the British medical profession in that year voluntarily reduced its prescribing. The main amphetamines are presently included in Class B of the 1971 Misuse of Drugs Act, and therefore unauthorised possession etc. carries the same penalties as for cannabis. Injectable amphetamines are in Class A of the Act. In 1983, 2,008 people were found guilty or cautioned for offences involving amphetamines, mostly unlawful possession.

Barbiturates are in many ways the opposite of amphetamines. They are sedatives or depressants with many similarities to alcohol in their effects, and have been often used to reduce insomnia and anxiety. Although most users of therapeutic doses do not develop significant tolerance or physical dependence, both of these effects are common with consumption of greater amounts. According to the Canadian Government's Commission of Inquiry[14] of 1970;

'The barbiturates have considerable potential for producing psychological and physiological dependence, and are probably second only to alcohol in frequency of drug-induced debilitation in modern society'.

They have also been said to be 'In many ways... more pernicious than heroin'[17]. Young[15], writing in 1971, estimated that at that time the number of individuals dependent on barbiturates in Britain was between 75,000 and 125,000, with non-dependent regular users numbering between 400,000 and 600,000.

Barbiturates have an extremely high overdose potential and have been the toxic agents in thousands of accidental or intentional deaths annually. In Britain between 1958 and 1962, the average number a year attributable to barbiturate poisoning was 1,020[15]. Isbell, quoted as 'the outstanding authority' on barbiturate misuse and dangers, argues that;

'the manifestations of chronic barbiturate intoxication are, in most ways, much more serious than those of addiction to morphine. Morphine causes much less impairment to mental ability and emotional control, and produces no motor inco-ordination... Withdrawal of morphine is much less dangerous than is withdrawal of barbiturates'.

Heavy consumption of barbiturates can cause 'irritability, aggressive behaviour, paranoid ideas, and self injury'[18].

Yet, whilst the dangers of these drugs became increasingly obvious in the 1950s and 60s, medical practitioners still prescribed them in enormous quantities. In 1970 an official D.H.S.S. Report[19] noted that 'there is abundant evidence that doctors prescribe barbiturates in large quantities without much regard for the risks which attend their use'. In that year about twelve million prescriptions for these drugs were written. More recently the activities of the Campaign on Use and Restriction of Barbiturates (CURB) have brought about a significant reduction in the provision of these drugs, although four million prescriptions were still issued in 1979.

Whilst it is true that very belatedly these sedatives have been largely, though not completely, replaced by alternatives such as 'Valium' (which are themselves not without serious problems and critics), it is important to note here the very minimal official and general concern which existed for many years about these particularly widely used and potentially dangerous drugs. Although the Home Secretary has recently widened the scope of the Misuse of Drugs Act to include barbiturates, for decades after their dangers became apparent they remained virtually uncontrolled by the drug laws. Their inclusion in the 1964 Drugs (Prevention of Misuse) Bill, did not occur because 'misuse of these drugs on their own... did not then appear to present a serious problem'[19], and 'in the absence of police or other evidence of social dangers arising from misuse, it was decided to take no action'[20]. But according to the 1970 D.H.S.S. Report[19] 'Of all people aged 15 and over who died from all causes in England and Wales in 1962, barbiturates killed 1 in 441 men, and 1 in 306 women'. In the same Report it was estimated that in 1959 there were approximately 110,000 cases of barbiturate poisoning. Clearly there has been an enormous discrepancy between the attitude to barbiturates and the attention given to the other drugs mentioned above.

ALCOHOL AND TOBACCO

Yet, of all the dependence-producing drugs consumed in this country, the one which is most widespread in its use, and the cause of extensive harm, is comparatively uncontrolled. Most official and popular concentration is on illegal drugs such as heroin and cannabis, but as Glatt[21] notes 'certainly the most widely used and misused drug (apart from nicotine) is alcohol, and the most widespread form of both psychological and physiological drug dependence is alcoholism'.

As already mentioned alcohol has many similarities with the barbiturates, but whilst the latter are legally only available on prescription (although this has not in practice been a severe limitation on their use and abuse), alcohol is regulated in only a limited way and is generally freely available to most people, many of whom would not even think of it as a 'drug' at all. Use itself, except by those aged under 18, is not controlled, only certain public consequences such as drunkenness and driving whilst under its influence. Yet, like barbiturates and some of the other drugs already considered, it is potentially and in reality very destructive and addictive. Kendell[2] has noted that 'ethanol is a drug of dependence like heroin or amylobarbitone and differs from them only in that much larger quantities have to be ingested for much longer before physical dependence develops'. The critical amount seems to be a daily intake of about 15cl. (120g.) of ethanol - equivalent to the alcohol in seven pints of beer or half a bottle of spirits - ingested over a period of several months. Shaw[22] has however argued that 'withdrawal symptoms occur in a very mild form after relatively small doses of alcohol' and that 'it is impossible to discern an easy cut-off point at which addiction "starts" '. This latter point is common to all dependence-producing drugs.

The problematic nature of alcohol is well summed up by Glatt[21], Vice-Chairman of the Medical Council on Alcoholism:

'from the aspects of dosage, length of time of administration, and the proportion of users who develop dependence, alcohol would be a less serious dependence-producing agent than barbiturates, and these in turn less so than the opiates. From the point of view of damage to health, however, the physical complications following excessive drinking may be more dangerous than those occurring after misuse of barbiturates and opiates; and the danger to life of acute alcohol or barbiturate withdrawal in very heavy drinkers and barbiturate addicts respectively may be greater than those from the withdrawal of the drug in opiate addicts'.

The number of 'alcoholics' or 'problem drinkers' in this country is hard to estimate, but a conservative estimate would be about 300,000, whilst other sources, including the Royal College of Psychiatrists[23], suggest over 700,000. Sir George Young, a Government Minister of Health, estimated a rise from 490,000 alcoholics in 1957 to 740,000 in 1977[21]. It has also been suggested that 'half of all murders, two-thirds of attempted suicides, a third of child abuse cases, a third of fatal road accidents and 80 per cent of deaths from fire are all connected with alcohol'[24]. After heart disease and cancer, alcoholism has been rated as the greatest cause of death in Britain, and in June 1980 Patrick Jenkin, Secretary of State at the D.H.S.S., commented that 'something like 1 in 25 of the population in England and Wales, and much higher in Scotland and Northern Ireland, maybe 1 in 10... may be personally affected by severe alcohol-related problems...', if account is taken of the effects on family and friends, as well as the actual sufferer[21].

Yet, whilst over the last twenty years government and official policies have become more aware of and concerned with alcoholism as an individual and social problem, their actual actions and provisions have been very limited indeed for such an apparently severe situation. Alcohol and its misuse is overshadowed in public and official interest by other types of drug use and dependence, but the problems created by the former, partly because of the extent of its use, are in reality very much greater. The official policy towards alcohol and alcoholism has remained ambiguous, with no critical and condemnatory reaction similar to that against drugs such as heroin and cannabis. Indeed, the government has been accused of prevarication and lack of concern over this issue. For example, in March 1982 the Department of Health was accused of suppressing health policies intended to combat growing alcohol misuse in Britain. In a leading article in the British Journal of Addiction, a number of psychiatrists and health campaigners expressed their anger at the Government's refusal to publish a two volume report on alcohol policies[25]. This report, finally published in Sweden, detailed a huge rise in drinking among adults between 1957 and 1977, and stated that more than 700,000 people suffered from severe drink problems. Seven main recommendations were made, none of which have been implemented. These included linking the tax on alcohol to the retail price index, development of policies aimed at keeping drinking at present levels per capita, more restrictions on liquor licencing, and tougher laws on drinking and driving.

Instead of publishing this document, the Social Services Secretary, Mr. Norman Fowler, substituted a report called 'Drinking Sensibly'[26], in which it is argued;

'The Government must... have regard to the economic importance of the drinks industry and the licenced trade and to the interests of those working in them. It is necessary to balance the arguments; to consider with care all the effects of measures designed to limit the harm caused by alcohol misuse; and to ensure that such measures do not have a disproportionate outcome for employment and trade or the social behaviour of the majority.'

In conclusion, the chapter 'Preventing alcohol misuse - the way forward', states:

'The precise role the Government should play in helping prevent alcohol misuse is clearly open to debate... Many people would resist the suggestion that the degree to which people choose to put their health at risk through their drinking habits is a legitimate interest of Government. And it has to be faced that Government controls capable of effectively influencing the minority who misuse alcohol could not be established without affecting the choices available to the majority of the population who drink sensibly. Also, while the misuse of alcohol may cause serious health and social problems, the production of and trade in alcoholic drinks form an important part of our economy in terms of jobs, exports, investment, and as a source of revenue for the Government - all of which could be adversely affected by any measures designed to restrict consumption'.

A similar position was expressed by Mr. Geoffrey Finsberg, a junior Health Minister, in December 1982 when he suggested that in the area of alcohol abuse, the key to preventing misuse is for individuals to accept responsibility for their own health, that a paternalistic attitude cannot be adopted, and that a national preventive strategy must reinforce personal responsibility[27].

In the same month, Mr. Fowler said 'Our aim is to alert the country to the dangers of allowing the problem of drug misuse to grow and spread. Our overriding policy is first to contain it, and then to reduce it. Drug misuse can destroy talents which should be put to the use of the community'[28].

Whilst it is clear that the official attitude to alcohol and alcoholism, for political, social and economic reasons, has been one of substantial inaction, the reaction to tobacco consumption and addiction has been, and is especially so at present, even more limited and dilatory. But whereas most drinking remains fairly unproblematic in its consequences, the same cannot be said of smoking, for few people once they start the latter habit can avoid physical addiction to it and subsequent health damage[29].

According to Plant[5], 'Cigarette smoking is very likely to produce dependence. Tobacco dependence is the most widespread form of drug dependence in the world'. Further, the severe and often fatal health risks have been apparent for over twenty years. Since at least the early 1960s, the Royal College of Physicians of London, in particular, has consistently shown the extreme damage that smoking causes and has argued for proper Governmental recognition of the seriousness of the situation. Its first report on smoking, 'Smoking and Health'[30], published in 1962, stated:

'The evidence that cigarette smoking often has harmful and dangerous consequences is now so convincing that preventive measures are undoubtedly needed'.

In the second report[31] of 1971 it was however regretted that 'the Government, although stating in 1962 that they accepted the evidence on the dangers of cigarette smoking, has taken no effective action to curtail the habit', whilst it was noted in 'Smoking OR Health'[29] that the steps taken by Government had remained paltry and hesitating. This latter report concluded:

'More determined action is needed. Activities directed against cigarette smoking in the United Kingdom have been relatively feeble... Such action must receive greater priority in plans for prevention of diseases. The health professions await a firmer lead from the Government to ensure that the people of this country will, by refraining from smoking, come to enjoy cleaner air, better health, and longer lives.'

In the most recent report[32], published in 1983 the Royal College goes so far as to accuse the Government of having an 'attitude of inactivity and encouragement towards the tobacco industry'.

Whilst tobacco sales have declined during the last ten years - due mainly to some public acceptance of the medical evidence - there are still at present between 16 and 17 million smokers in this country, who bought over 102,000 million cigarettes in 1982. Their drug is estimated to account for between 15 to 20 per cent of all British deaths, with the annual death toll from tobacco use estimated at not less than 100,000. In 1981 there were about 70,000 deaths from lung cancer, bronchitis, and obstructive lung disease, of which over 90 per cent can be attributed to tobacco smoking[32].

Although there are some limited voluntary agreements between the tobacco industry and Government, there is no legislation in the United Kingdom restricting or controlling tobacco sales or smoking, with the exception of that banning cigarette advertising on television and the sale of tobacco to children, the latter being hardly ever enforced. As Secretary of State for Social Services, Sir Keith Joseph stated that legislation against cigarettes was 'a significant and dangerous diminution of corporate and personal freedom'[33], whilst more recently, in 1981, Geoffrey Finsberg, junior Health Minister, declared;

'My government does not welcome the use of regulatory or legislative measures in order to control the legitimate commercial freedom of tobacco companies'[33].

This issue of freedom and objections to the 'encroachments of the Nanny State' are often used, especially by Conservatives, in justification of inaction in this area. However, the Office of Population Censuses and Surveys has recently shown that many smokers remain unconvinced that smoking will adversely affect their health, 44% justifying their lack of concern with the argument that if smoking was really dangerous then the government would ban advertising[34].

As Daube, former national director of Action on Smoking and Health (ASH) points out,

'The Government's double standards become all too clear when one compares inaction on smoking with the very real progress being made on solvent abuse... But in Scotland in the years 1976-82 solvent abuse was responsible for 33 deaths: cigarette smoking was responsible over the same period for 63,000 deaths, as well as much avoidable ill health'[35].

There have nevertheless been some notable and worthy exceptions within governments, both Conservative and Labour, who have tried hard and extensively to bring about restrictions on the tobacco industry in the interests of public health. All of them have been thwarted on political or economic grounds. Control of smoking, like drinking, has always been seen rightly or wrongly by political parties as a sure way of achieving electoral hostility - an interesting contrast to anticipated popular condemnation of attempts to reduce control or penalties on illegal drug-taking such as cannabis use. Of the relevant Ministers, the case of Sir George Young, junior Health Minister in the 1979 Conservative Government, is of the most interest, as many people believe he was forced from office because of tobacco company pressure. Taylor[33], in his book on the politics of tobacco, has written:

'Unlike Labour's Health Ministers, Kenneth Robinson and Dr David Owen, who favoured legislation to restrict advertising, Sir George favoured a total ban on all cigarette advertising and sponsorship. Dismissing arguments about revenue, jobs and trade, he pushed ahead, determined to destroy the industry's power to perpetuate its myth about cigarettes. Sir George put public health first. But in doing so, he aroused opposition within his own party, not just from tobacco's known supporters, but from many Conservative backbenchers who embraced the industry's argument that Sir George was attacking freedom not cigarettes. Mrs Thatcher moved him before damage was done, and replaced him with a Minister who posed the industry little threat'.

The Home Secretary did not allude to the multi-national tobacco corporations when, in December 1983, he condemned drug traffickers who 'make fortunes out of the misery of addiction'[36]. Their respectable veneer and contributions of £4 billion a year in tax to Government coffers apparently allows them to be excluded when such unsavoury groups are attacked!

CONTRADICTIONS IN OFFICIAL POLICIES

What should now be clear is the existence of a definite dichotomy in the perceptions of and policy responses to drugs which chemically often produce very similar effects; it might be suggested that some of the most dangerous drugs are tolerated most. It is possible to argue that, practically, the attitudes to alcohol and alcoholism, and possibly also tobacco and its use, are not altogether unreasonable or unrealistic. Certainly, individual health problems have to be considered in relation to benefits and liberties - personal, social and economic - in the community. But such an understanding is not extended, as surely logically it should be, to the field of illegal drugs where a monolithic, critical and dogmatic position rules supreme. There is no acceptance here that it may not be a legitimate interest of Government to interfere if people choose to put their health at risk nor is it accepted that even if the use of some drugs may cause serious health and other problems, other factors, equivalent to the economic and employment ones relevant to alcohol and tobacco, must also be taken into consideration. These include the exacerbation of the problems and misery which some drug users experience by the criminalisation of the drug-taking activities; the continuing strength given to the black market and organised crime, ironically created by attempts to control illegal drug administration; the disrespect with which the law generally comes to be held, particularly by young black people, when especially the law against cannabis possession is enforced and the powers of search misused; the corruption of police officers and others, which is potentially always present and was in fact so a few years ago in the Metropolitan police drugs squad, arises from the incredible criminal profits to be made from trafficking in illegal drugs. There is no acceptance that most illegal drugs, like alcohol, can be sensibly and fairly harmlessly used, rather than always abused. There is no concession that the role the Government can itself play in encouraging a sensible attitude to drug-taking is still open to debate, nor that it is necessary to balance the arguments.

EXPLANATIONS AND DISCUSSION OF OFFICIAL POLICIES

It is apparent from the discussion so far that the separation of drugs into legal and illegal categories cannot be supported by considerations of their chemical 'dangerousness' or 'addictiveness', nor by their actual or potential damage to individuals or society. On the one hand, as we have seen, drugs such as alcohol, tobacco and barbiturates can all produce physical dependence and be extremely destructive to health, yet are or have been relatively uncontrolled, and their use has not incurred the concern and condemnation which might reasonably be expected. On the other hand, cannabis is neither an addictive drug nor an obviously harmful one, but is severely and punitively controlled, resulting in the harassment and criminalisation of many people each year. Whilst heroin and amphetamines can be problematic drugs, at worst they seem to be no more harmful, and, when not complicated by the conditions which arise from their illegal status, may be less dangerous or destructive than many of the legal substances in general use.

Nor do attempts to analyse the responses to particular drugs in terms of non-medical or recreational 'abuse' versus medical or therapeutic use help us to any extent. It is true that the reaction against heroin and amphetamines developed quickly after it was observed that these drugs were being increasingly used recreationally, a point which will be returned to, but alcohol and tobacco, the major recreational drugs, are not condemned, except by a very small minority, because they are used for non-therapeutic purposes.

How, then, are we to account for these apparently inconsistent and contradictory responses to drugs which are often very similar in their effects? Certainly, historical accident and economic considerations should not be underestimated. These are clearly important for understanding the continuing acceptance of alcohol and tobacco use. Nor can the significant dangers which some drugs do pose be completely ruled out as irrelevant. But these points cannot provide a complete and adequate explanation, as they cannot account for the severity of the response to at least some types of drugs and their use.

Another pattern can be identified which explains these varied reactions. In practice, in spite of all the statements that justify intervention on the grounds of the dangerousness of illegal drugs and the protection of individuals from harm, it is not so much the drugs themselves or their use as such which are condemned, but rather particular types of users and their attitudes and life-styles. As Young[15] has observed;

'It is the use of drugs in radically different ways to achieve ends condemned by powerful groups in society which... evokes reactions of a substantial and punitive nature'.

Similarly, Jaffe[37] has written:

'Firstly, a pattern of drug use is seen as a problem when it deviates from a traditionally accepted or an emerging cultural norm. And, secondly, it is seen as a problem when it impairs health or social functioning. The theme of deviance is one that is most salient to the definition of a drug problem, but deviance may or may not be associated with a threat to health.'

With this in mind, we can now reconsider the changing attitude to heroin and amphetamines, the continuing opposition to cannabis, and the complacency shown to the use of the barbiturates, alcohol and tobacco.

As we have seen, opiate dependence in the decades before 1960 was predominantly restricted to 'therapeutic' addicts or to members of the medical profession, and was considered to be a marginal problem of little concern. Such passive drug use fitted fairly easily into the established norm and posed no threat. However, this changed significantly with the emergence of a new, younger and less orthodox type of addict in the 1960s. Their use of heroin was more hedonistic, in Rolleston's terms 'a vicious indulgence', and their addiction was often flaunted as a 'master status', symbolising their general rejection of conventional and accepted values. It was these latter unorthodox cultural patterns and systems of meaning which were opposed by what Duster[38] has called the 'moral center', although intervention was legitimated through the manifestation of concern about the dangers of such drug use.

Indeed, the health problems and dangerousness arising from the use of heroin were probably exacerbated quite considerably by the extension of criminalisation to the behaviour of these new addicts. If the damaging consequences of their drug use had been of primary concern, then a more apt alternative reaction aimed at a minimisation of harm could have been expected. A continuation of this interpretation is probably still valid for the present day, with its more widespread heroin use, although it has to be acknowledged that the full meaning of the current situation is not yet clear. Whilst the new users are less mobile and seem to be less obviously socially marginalised, with life-styles less clearly oppositional, nevertheless their euphoria-seeking heroin use, which seems to be substantially a response to the bleak conditions of chronic unemployment and purposelessness in our communities, is of a quite different type from the stable and unobtrusive use of the old therapeutic addicts. Official reaction still centres around criminal justice intervention against the users, and their use is enforced as a master-status, even if not seen by the individuals as such. This enables their 'problematic' behaviour and rejection of, or withdrawal from, conventional roles to be explained away at the individual level of pathology, allowing the structural and social conditions which in many cases encourage this type of drug use as a meaningful choice (though not usually a positive one) to be hidden and ignored. Dorn[39] has argued that in a situation of planned unemployment where little or nothing can be done to create jobs on a permanent basis, the structural and political reasons for the failure of many young people to obtain jobs can be rationalised through seeing unemployed youth as individuals messed-up through drug use. He has written that;

' "drug problems" in the teenage working class were, in the sixties, a matter for concern because they appeared to threaten the transition from school to work. But now, in a period of increased unemployment, the drug problem offers one non-structural explanation for failure to make that transition'.

Similarly, the Drugs (Prevention of Misuse) Act of 1964, which made it an offence to be in unauthorised possession of amphetamines, was introduced after 'mounting public concern over the increasing misuse by young persons of drugs containing amphetamine... was reflected in Questions in Parliament and in articles in the press and elsewhere'[19]. Laurie[17] has persuasively argued that the campaign against amphetamines appeared to be an attempt by adult society to seize on something concrete in the apparent morass of changing adolescent standards. Whilst controlling legislation was quick to follow the revelation of 'hedonistic' use of amphetamines, there was little concern about the extensive and sometimes dangerously excessive 'legitimate' prescription of both these drugs and the barbiturates to mainly middle-aged housewives who found their lives disappointingly unglamorous and emotionally barren. Yet, as Laurie says, there was a lot of similarity between the 'sadly bored and understimulated' lives of both groups. What was being condemned, then, seems to be the professionally uncontrolled and oppositional attempts by some young people to alter their situations themselves and achieve some excitement in otherwise constrained existences. Amphetamine use was acceptable when it supported conventional values and enabled approved but routine or tedious tasks to be tolerated, but was unacceptable when consumed in weekend sprees to stay awake at all-night parties and such like, even when this latter use did not result in any apparent harm.

The continuous condemnation of cannabis use makes this cultural and generational conflict even more clear. In the main, this drug at least in the recent past has been very attractive to those who reject the materialistic values and aggressiveness of society. Writing in 1967, Silberman (quoted in Laurie[17]) noted;

'In ideological terms it would be true to say that it is the drug of those whose general orientation is anti-authoritarian, anti-militaristic and, in the context of contemporary Western societies, anti-establishment'.

Plant[40] also found that many of the drug-takers he encountered were 'discontented with the social order'. Generally, his study group was 'radical, or uncommitted to conventional or traditional political and religious outlooks'. More recently a racial element has also been introduced in that many young West Indians believe that cannabis use is an integral and acceptable aspect of their culture. This clearly conflicts with more established British attitudes.

Attacks on this drug hide a much wider and more complex conflict in which in supposedly democratic and pluralistic societies, it would be more difficult for the authorities legitimately and openly to intervene. As Young has observed, marihuana has been a perfect weapon, since suspicion of use justifies harassment and arrest of members of cultures and groups which are disapproved of. It should therefore come as no surprise that the extensive search powers of the police have often not achieved finds of drugs - the average success rate of searches which have been officially recorded has been about 25%, whilst one force has been noted for obtaining less than 4% - for in practice it seems that the real purpose is not primarily to control drugs, but to enable a show of strength by the established order and to contain the resistance of deviants and members of 'problem' populations. Furthermore, this view that it is not solely the drug but specific cultures which are the objects of intervention helps to explain the hysterical and intolerant reaction by Parliament and the media against the reasonable but hardly radical Wootton Report on Cannabis. Its careful refutation of cannabis as an addictive drug, or one the use of which would inevitably lead to heroin addiction, was almost completely ignored. The Shadow Home Secretary insisted that 'the addicts of hashish and marihuana' should be pursued 'with the utmost severity that the law allows'[12], whilst James Callaghan, the Home Secretary, was vehement and insulting in his criticisms of the Report, seeing it as over-influenced by 'a lobby in favour of legalising cannabis'. According to 'The Times', he saw this as 'another aspect of the permissive society and he was glad that his decision had enabled the House to call a halt to the advancing tide of permissiveness'[15]. The fact that the Report rejected legalisation and argued merely for a reduction in maximum penalties seems not to have been of any importance in the debate - indeed, most of its findings were ignored in the rush to heap condemnation on it. As pointed out earlier, Government opposition to this drug is still strong, although there is some feeling that its critics are now more moderate and that legalisation or decriminalisation is more possible now than previously. If this is the case, however, it has not resulted from any greater knowledge of the substance but rather from a change both in the type of users and in the meaning given to their use. Such change is probably also the basis of the recent less severe reaction by the courts to those found guilty of possessing this drug.

In contrast, the complacent or complex attitudes to the use of and damage caused by alcohol, tobacco, and the legal pharmaceuticals, can be partly explained by their structurally non-threatening use by the conventional and consensual majority of the population. Legal drug taking can be seen as 'behaviour in tune with the values of society', which helps to keep the system functioning[15]. Drugs which are either supportive of the present social structure - economically or through their effects on individuals - or which have now become established and their use routine through social practice, are tolerated if not encouraged, with their use being seen as problematic or an 'abuse' only in extreme situations.

In conclusion, the State's response to drugs is not coherent at the level of addictiveness, or even potential dangerousness, and it has to be accepted that these do not appear to be the main grounds for official concern and intervention against certain drugs and their users. Instead, along with economic considerations, it seems that the status and attitudes of users, and the purposes and meaning of their use, are of central importance in determining the reactions to drugs. Unfortunately, if my arguments are correct, it would seem to be optimistic to expect a significant and rational reconsideration of the area, since so many social conflicts and emotional responses are involved. Nevertheless, some call for a more rational understanding and consistent response must be made. We need to break away from stereotypical and simplistic views of drugs, often fostered by Governments and the media, and instead approach the area differently. We must argue for policies which reasonably deal with legal and illegal drugs together, and which appreciate that not all illegal drugs and their use are necessarily problematic or damaging to any extent, whilst also accepting that many legal drugs, athough often beneficial, are capable of being individually and socially very destructive. Moves must be made away from the conception that the mere use of certain types of drugs is the essential problem, towards concentration on minimising the damage which can result from most drugs when used unwisely.

Further, the intentions underlying interventions against certain types of drug use must be clearly defined, and it should be understood that in practice policies which intend to control problematic drug consumption may, due to the complexities of the area, create generally more harm than good. Of course, it is to be expected that opposition against certain groups in society will continue, but if the drug-related grounds disguising the real meaning of such interventions are taken away, then unjustifiable reactions may at least become more restricted or their real intentions more transparent.

Acknowledgement

I would like to thank Dr. Martin Plant for his kind and helpful comments on, and corrections to, the draft of this paper.

References

1. Thorley, A. & Plant, M. 'Misuse of Drugs' in McCreadie, R.G. *Rehabilitation in Psychiatric Practice*. Pitman, London, 1982.

2. Kendell, R.E. 'Alcoholism: a medical or a political problem?' *British Medical Journal* 1, 1979.

3. Jaffe, J.H. 'Drug Addiction and Drug Misuse' in Goodman, L.S. (Ed.) Goodman and Gilman's *The Pharmacological Basis of Therapeutics*. Macmillan, New York, 1980.

4. Stimson, G.V. *Heroin and Behaviour*. Irish University Press, Shannon, 1973.

5. Plant, M.A. *Drugs in Perspective*. Hodder and Stoughton, Sevenoaks, 1981.

6. *Departmental Committee on Morphine and Heroin Addiction. Report*. H.M.S.O., London, 1926.

7. Bean, P. *The Social Control of Drugs*. Martin Robertson, London, 1974.

8. Stimson, G. & Oppenheimer. E. *Heroin Addiction - Treatment and Control in Britain*. Tavistock, London, 1982.

9. *The Times Law Report. R. v. Aramah* 18.12.82

10. Home Office. *Statistics of the Misuse of Drugs in the United Kingdom*, 1983 and Supplementary Tables 1983.

11. Advisory Committee on Drug Dependence. *Report on Cannabis*. H.M.S.O., London, 1968.

12. Schofield, M. *The Strange Case of Pot*. Penguin, Harmondsworth, 1971.

13. *The Times*. 12.4.84.

14. Canadian Government Commission of Inquiry. *The Non-Medical Use of Drugs - Interim Report*. Penguin, Harmondsworth, 1971.

15. Young, J. *The Drugtakers*. MacGibbon & Kee, London, 1971.

16. Brecher, E.M. and the Editors of Consumer Reports. *Licit and Illicit Drugs*. Little, Brown & Co., Boston, 1972.

17. Laurie, P. *Drugs*. Penguin, Harmondsworth, 1971.

18. Lewis, A.J. *Amphetamines, Barbiturates, LSD and Cannabis*. H.M.S.O., London, 1970.

19. Advisory Committee on Drug Dependence. *Report on the Amphetamines and Lysergic Acid Diethylamide (LSD)*. H.M.S.O., London, 1970.

20. Communication from Home Office, Narcotics Branch, 26.8.66, quoted in Laurie[17].

21. Glatt, M.M. *Alcoholism*. Hodder and Stoughton, Sevenoaks, 1982.

22. Shaw, S. 'What is Problem Drinking?' in Plant, M.A. (Ed.) *Drinking and Problem Drinking*. Junction Books, London, 1982.

23. Royal College of Psychiatrists. *Alcohol and Alcoholism*. Tavistock, London, 1979.

24. *The Scotsman*. 15.9.83

25. *The Guardian*. 31.3.82

26. Department of Health and Social Security. *Prevention and Health: Drinking Sensibly*. H.M.S.O., London, 1981.

27. *The Economist*. 4.12.82

28. *The Times*. 2.12.82

29. The Royal College of Physicians of London. *Smoking OR Health: Third Report*. Pitman Medical, London, 1977.

30. The Royal College of Physicians of London. *Smoking and Health.* Pitman Medical, London, 1962.

31. The Royal College of Physicians of London. *Smoking and Health Now: Second Report.* Pitman Medical, London, 1971.

32. The Royal College of Physicians of London. *Health or Smoking: Fourth Report.* Pitman Medical, London, 1983.

33. Taylor, P. *Smoke Ring - The Politics of Tobacco.* Bodley Head, London, 1984.

34. ASH - *Supporters' News.* No. 1. Winter 1983/84.

35. Letter to *The Guardian.* 30.12.83

36. *The Scotsman.* 15.12.83.

37. Jaffe, J. 'What Counts as a "Drug Problem"?' in Edwards, G., Arif, A. & Jaffe, J. (Eds.) *Drug Use and Misuse - Cultural Perspectives.* Croom Helm, London, 1983.

38. Duster, T. *The Legislation of Morality.* The Free Press, New York, 1970.

39. Dorn, N. 'The Conservatism of the Cannabis Debate' in National Deviancy Conference (Ed.). *Permissiveness and Control.* Macmillan, London, 1980.

40. Plant, M.A. *Drugtakers in an English Town.* Tavistock, London, 1975.